Beyond Adventure

Beyond Adventure

The Lives of Three Explorers

by

ROY CHAPMAN ANDREWS

New York

Duell, Sloan and Pearce

Seventh Printing August, 1958

The lines by Robert Service are reprinted by permission of
Dodd, Mead & Company from *Collected Poems of Robert
Service.*

*Published simultaneously in Canada
by Little, Brown & Company (Canada) Limited*

PRINTED IN THE UNITED STATES OF AMERICA

This book is dedicated with admiration
and affection to the memory of my friend
WILLIAM HERBERT HOBBS
Greenland explorer, inspiring teacher,
distinguished student of glaciology,
mountain climber, and eminent biographer.

The trails of the world be countless, and most of the trails be tried;
You tread on the heels of the many, till you come where the ways divide;
And one lies safe in the sunlight, and the other is dreary and wan,
Yet you look aslant at the Lone Trail, and the Lone Trail lures you on.

— ROBERT W. SERVICE

Contents

Acknowledgments

D URING 1952–1953 these streamlined biographies were written for *True,* the Man's Magazine. I have had many requests from libraries and individuals to put them together in a book where they would be more permanent and easily accessible. The editors of *True* have kindly allowed me to do so.

When I was about to write the piece on Admiral Peary, I asked my old friend, the late Dr. William Herbert Hobbs, if I might use information which he had gathered for his carefully documented biography entitled *Peary.* He replied, "I am delighted and complimented."

My thanks are also due to his publishers, The Macmillan Company, New York. They have kindly supplemented Dr. Hobbs's permission to use some of the material of his book.

I have had access, also, to the personal, unpublished diary of the late George Borup, one of the staff of the successful North Pole expedition of 1908–1909.

ROY CHAPMAN ANDREWS

Prologue

THIS book tells the life stories of three men, Robert E. Peary, Carl Akeley, and myself. Although as different as the countries in which they were lived, yet in essentials the stories have much in common. We were all explorers: Peary in geography, Akeley in natural history, and I in science. Each of us was impelled to do what he did do by an idea that took complete possession of his mind and being: an idea so dominant that, had he been unsuccessful, he would have considered his whole life to be a failure.

Peary's idea was to reach the North Pole; Akeley's to bring to America the vanishing wild life of Africa in all its truth and beauty; mine to explore Central Asia with a great scientific expedition.

The parents of each of the three of us were of moderate means, living in small country towns. No one of the parents dreamed that his son was born to be an explorer. Peary's mother expected him to practice engineering; Akeley's father hoped he would remain on the farm; my parents thought I might teach zoology. But, as I wrote in Peary's biography, "An explorer's ultimate destiny is determined by hereditary biological factors that will not be denied.

They eventually triumph over environment or circumstance, leading him to the path he was born to follow."

Peary joined the United States Navy as an engineer; Akeley and I went into natural history museums. Once launched in our professions, each of us passed through a period of preparation and maturation while the idea that eventually came to dominate his mind germinated and took final shape.

Each of us had a difficult struggle to finance his plan. Each of us went through periods of utter discouragement when it seemed that his dream could never materialize. Each of us felt the same spiritual uplift when he sailed for the land that held all his hope.

For Peary it meant sacrifice and incredible hardship. He spent twenty-three years in the Arctic before he attained his goal. There were heartbreaking separations from his wife and children. Punishment of his mind and body reached the uttermost limit of human endurance, yet he never thought of giving up. At the end, he sailed back to civilization "with the Pole on board."

Carl Akeley, in pursuit of his vision for African Hall, in the American Museum of Natural History, New York City, drove himself unmercifully. He died from sheer exhaustion in a little tent high on the slopes of Mt. Mikeno in the Congo, but with the knowledge that his dream had become reality. I know he was well content.

My job took me to the Gobi, one of the greatest and most arid deserts in the world. A land of desolation, of thirst and cold and parching heat, of sandstorms and mighty gales. But a land that gave richly of its treasures because we had the will to go and seek them.

What strange force impels a man to leave the comforts of civilization, home, and family to probe the wilderness? A primitive love of nature and of adventure is the primary reason; another is the spirit of inquiry. To the born explorer, adventure is a vital flame. Without it life would be a poor thing indeed. And the desire to see unknown lands, to discover new facts, becomes a resistless drive that will not be denied. No matter what the cost he must go. It gives him the ultimate satisfaction, a fulfillment and meaning to existence found nowhere else. In nature, he realizes himself and discovers truth and happiness.

Such a philosophy can be understood and appreciated by only a few, but it is as old as the human race. Man's most primitive grandfather was an explorer. Some member of the tribe felt the inborn urge to see what lay beyond the horizon's rim. He found new hunting grounds and led his people to other valleys. Thus the world today is known to the uttermost limit, and man has become master of the earth and the sea and the air.

The old days of the Arctic explorer foot-slogging behind his sled, or of camel caravans plodding across the desert, are gone. Airplanes and jeeps have taken their place. Today there remain but a few small spots on the world's map unmarked by explorer's trails, or where an airplane has not droned above the mountain peaks — only a few small areas whose topographical features are unknown.

But that does not mean the end of exploration. It means only that the problems and the methods have changed. There are still vast regions potentially unknown, and some hold undreamed of treasures in the realm of science. To study these areas; to reveal the history of their making; to learn what they can give for education, culture and human welfare — that is the exploration of the present and the future on the surface of this planet. But in the limitless realm of outer space, in the uttermost depths of the sea and the caverns of the earth, the explorer has new worlds to conquer. Man will never rest until he knows their secrets.

"I Shall Find a Way
or Make One"

ON April 6, 1909, Robert E. Peary stood at the mathematical point on the earth's surface where North and South, East and West blend into one. For more than two decades he had fought to reach that spot. Year after year when he said good-by to his wife and children, the thought in his mind was that he might never see them again. Hunger, searing cold, punishment of mind and body to uttermost human endurance awaited him in the unknown desolation of snow and ice. Yet an almost fanatical dedication to the service of an idea drove him on.

During his worst moments of depression, he never thought of giving up. When he lay in Greely's abandoned camp at Fort Conger, suffering the agonies of the damned from frozen feet, facing the ruin of all his hopes, he wrote on the cabin wall his guiding motto — the line from Seneca: *Inveniam viam aut faciam* (I shall find a way or make one).

No explorer since Christopher Columbus had clung so tenaciously to an ideal, or suffered so much because of it, as Robert E. Peary. On that April day in 1909 at the top of the world, he wrote in his diary: "The Pole at last. The prize of three centuries. My dream and goal for twenty years. Mine at last! I cannot bring myself to realize it. It seems so simple and commonplace."

After thirty hours at the Pole for sun observations, he

started back. Fortune and superb planning favored him. Fifteen days later, on April 22nd, he stood on land again, and the next day reached the base camp at Cape Columbia. Forty-eight hours of sleep, then on to the *Roosevelt*, frozen in the pack ninety-two miles away. With "the Pole on board," the ship steamed southward to what every man expected would be deserved acclaim for a job well done.

But at the first village on the Greenland coast they heard disturbing news. The Eskimos told them that Dr. Frederick A. Cook, who Peary knew was in the Arctic, had returned early in the spring and said he had gone far north. But the natives shook their heads: "That is not true. He lied. Two of our tribe were with him."

At Etah the report was confirmed. Peary, and others of his party, talked with Itukishoo and Apilah, Cook's Eskimo companions. They stoutly maintained that they had been only two marches out on the sea ice, and not beyond sight of land. Although he never expected to need them, Peary obtained their signed statements. He examined, also, one of the two light sledges Cook had used. Obviously, it had not traveled over much rough sea ice.

When the *Roosevelt* reached Indian Harbor, Labrador, and was in touch with the world, Peary heard that a cablegram from Lerwick in the Shetland Islands stated that Dr. Cook had reached the North Pole on April 21, 1908, and was then *en route* to Copenhagen on the little Danish steamer *Hans Egele*. Knowing the facts, it seemed incredible that Cook dared make such a claim. Peary and his men could not believe that Cook's tale would be accepted at face value by the world. Peary wired the United Press: "Cook's story should not be taken too seriously. Two Eskimos who accompanied him say he went no distance north and not out of sight of land. Other tribesmen corroborate."

On the *Roosevelt* indignation mounted. Peary composed another telegram, for the *New York Times,* which he brought to the mess room where the men were sitting. "Is it too strong?" he asked. "No, no," they shouted. Then Borup remarked, "Why don't you say he has handed the public a gold brick? That's what he's done."

MacMillan writes of this: "He, Peary, called me to his room and asked: 'What is a synonym for gold brick?' 'I don't know,' I replied. 'As far as I know there is no word just like it in the English language.'

" 'It is an ugly word,' he added. 'I don't like to use it. Let's think it over for awhile!'

"We did and failed and so he wrote the radiogram which hurt him more than it did Cook."

The World's Greatest Hoax

These cables heralded the greatest and most enduring hoax ever perpetrated on the world by one man. It saddened the life of a heroic American, probably prevented the Stars and Stripes from flying first at the South Pole — by making impossible an expedition planned by Peary with Captain Bartlett in command — and made "debunking" of explorers a favorite pastime for a generation. The Cook-Peary controversy was the most bitter and virulent nonpolitical argument ever known in America. It developed into a veritable orgy of public and private wrangling that reached the bounds of hysteria.

The most influential newspapers in the land sided either with Cook or Peary as definitely as in any political campaign. The question was argued in country stores, in city clubs, in the halls of Congress and in private homes. It caused divorces, broken friendships and disruption of families. And recently, forty-three years after the two men came out of the Arctic, the controversy has been revived by the posthumous publication of a book by Frederick A. Cook, *Return from the Pole*.

It is incredible how the thing lasts. Tempers still flare at the mere mention of Cook *vs*. Peary. Only a short time ago, while I was speaking at a dinner given to the former presidents of the Explorers Club in New York City, a guest leaped to his feet and denounced me in violent language for "defaming" Cook's character — and this after Cook, as the result of an oil scandal, had served a term in Leavenworth penitentiary for using the mails to defraud investors.

When Cook's claim was discredited by every reputable geographic society at home and abroad, it seemed only to add fuel to the blazing fire. The newspapers that espoused Cook either would not publish such news at all, or tucked it in an obscure corner inside the least-read portion. The populace knew little about what sort of records an explorer was supposed to keep and cared less. They had taken their position and to hell with the facts. The controversy had reached the point of unreasoning mass hysteria.

Why the Public Accepted Cook

After four decades it is interesting to analyze the reasons for this extraordinary public attitude. They are not obscure. During three hundred years the North Pole had been the greatest prize for Arctic explorers. The race was keen among many hardy men of many nations. In America, Peary was the foremost contestant, a famous explorer whose expeditions had been largely publicized. Cook was virtually unknown. The idea of the "little man" slipping off quietly into the Arctic with no fanfare and accomplishing alone, in one season, what Peary had tried to do for two decades caught the popular fancy. Then Peary played right into Cook's hands with his unfortunate telegrams from Labrador. Some years later, at the Explorers Club in New York, while we were sitting before the fire, alone, Peary said to me, "Andrews, I'd give anything if I hadn't sent those telegrams! If I had kept quiet, Cook would have ruined himself anyway, for he had no records to prove his claim."

But Peary's action was only human. After twenty-three years of suffering and hardship in an honest effort to reach the Pole, to have a man who he knew was a fraud steal the glory was more than he could bear. Nevertheless, in the public eyes Peary was branded as a poor sportsman who could not tolerate being beaten at his own game by a better explorer. A good mass psychologist, Cook was quick to take advantage of Peary's mistake. He only replied: "There is glory enough for all." Posing as a modest, simple little man, somewhat bewildered by the world's acclaim and honors, he capitalized on them to the ultimate

[7]

degree and with no delay. After an amazing initial welcome in Copenhagen, when king and commoner rushed to do him honor, he sailed for New York and a public reception cleverly staged by his supporters; then off on a whirlwind lecture tour across the continent. He spoke to crowds greater than in any but a political campaign, at high fees. The total receipts reached hundreds of thousands of dollars. Cook was a natural showman. He knew what the people wanted to hear and he gave it to them in large doses. His lectures dripped with thrills and harrowing stories of hardship and danger. They lapped it up. Cook was riding the crest of the wave. Dr. William Herbert Hobbs remarks, in his biography, *Peary*, that a popular vote conducted by a Pittsburgh newspaper as to who had reached the Pole gave Cook victory ten to one. The absurdity of such proceeding is evident, but no one cared that Cook had submitted no records of any kind to any geographical society, and that his claim rested entirely on his own word.

Peary Refuses Receptions or Awards

When Peary returned from the Arctic, he went immediately to his summer home at Eagle Island, Maine, to wait until his daily records and scientific data had been passed upon by a well-known geographical society. Thus Cook had a clear field in which to spread his propaganda, which he did with consummate skill.

Dr. Hobbs records that only once during this time did Peary appear in public. That was in October, in New York, at the great naval parade on the Hudson River celebrating the tercentenary of the voyage of Fulton's *Clermont*. He had promised that the *Roosevelt* could be included, and he would not break his word. Peary stood on the quarter-deck of the *Roosevelt* while insulting epithets and challenges came from well-organized Cook supporters on passing excursion boats. No one on the *Roosevelt* was allowed to make a reply. George Borup, one of the polar party, told me that never in his life had he endured such an ordeal and that for Peary it must have been absolute hell.

Within informed circles, Peary had enemies who were only too ready to support Cook and thus bring discredit to the man they disliked. The flame of unreasoning popular hysteria was fanned by certain well-known Arctic explorers, competitors of Peary, who were jealous of his success where some of them had failed. The great Nansen only grudgingly gave praise, and the Scandinavians Sverdrup, Rasmussen, and Amundsen actively supported Cook. Most important enemies of Peary in the United States were General A. W. Greely and Admiral W. S. Schley. In 1883, Greely, then a lieutenant with no Arctic experience, had commanded the Lady Franklin Bay Expedition which ended in awful tragedy. When a relief ship did not appear as scheduled, Greely and his party left their well-stocked base camp at Fort Conger in panic, thinking they would be cut off in the Arctic, and dashed southward to Cape Sabine on the Ellesmere Island coast, with inadequate supplies. There, many of the party died of starvation, and charges of cannibalism were hinted. Only seven out of twenty-four men remained alive to be rescued by Admiral Schley, then a commander in the Navy. One of the most dramatic evenings I ever spent was when I, as president of

[9]

the Explorers Club, with two others, read the heartbreaking letters to his wife found on the body of the doctor of the expedition. With the doctor's letters were his wife's last letters to him, received in Labrador on the way north. They are intimate revelations of two lonely souls: one a young girl facing long months of separation from her husband; the other a man slowly dying of starvation. In his account of the North Pole expedition written for *Hampton's* magazine, Peary said of Greely's Starvation Camp at Cape Sabine: "I first saw the place in August, 1896, in a blinding snowstorm. . . . I shall never forget the impression of that day — the pity and sickening sense of horror. The saddest part of the whole story for me, was the knowledge that the catastrophe was unnecessary, that it might have been avoided. I, and my men, have been cold, and have been near to starvation in the Arctic when cold and hunger were inevitable; but the horrors of Cape Sabine were not inevitable. They are a blot upon the record of American Arctic exploration."

Greely and Schley Lead Attack against Peary

Peary only told the bald truth, for musk oxen were within easy reach had Greely known where, and how to get them, and the men could have sledged back to Fort Conger. But this frank statement made Greely a bitter enemy. One day I came into the dining room of the Cosmos Club, in Washington, with Peary. At the lunch hour the place was crowded. As we stood in the doorway waiting for a table, General Greely rose from near the center of the room and said, in a voice that all could hear, "There is that dirty dog Peary. I won't eat in the same room with him."

Peary made no comment, and his face did not change expression; he simply continued our conversation where it had been interrupted.

My personal relations with Greely had been cordial, but after that day he never spoke, or wrote, to me again. I regretted this, for Greely had been president of the Explorers Club and was a charming man, but my association with Peary damned me in his eyes. Greely named "Schley Land" for his friend Admiral Schley, who had commanded the rescue ship, but Peary's explorations showed that it did not exist and geographers deleted it from their maps. Schley never forgave Peary for exposing this error, even though it was confirmed later by Admiral Byrd and other explorers.

Greely had considerable influence, and he worked actively to defame Peary and espouse Cook's cause. In 1910, when a bill was introduced in Congress to give Peary the thanks of Congress and retire him from the navy with the rank of rear admiral, Representative Macon spoke for an hour and forty minutes of almost unbelievable vituperation against Peary. He declared Peary's story to be "fake, pure and simple."

Peary endured these attacks silently and with characteristic dignity. All the leading geographical societies in the world had recognized his claim and many had awarded him medals. In Europe he had shared honors with another great American, Theodore Roosevelt, who had just returned from hunting in Africa. But he was still cruelly hurt, and his later life was saddened by the controversy that had arisen after twenty-three years of almost superhuman effort in the Arctic. Dr. Hobbs writes that when the University of Copenhagen, the only scientific body to whom Cook would submit his so-called "records," utterly repudiated Cook and his claims, the New York *Nation* carried an editorial which read: "As for Peary himself he has been defrauded of something which can never be restored to him. . . . Fake as it has been proved, the claim . . . has dimmed the lustre of the true discoverer's achievement. He will receive the full acknowledgement that his work merits in the form of recognition from scientific and other bodies and of a sure place in history; but the joy of the acclaim that should have greeted him at the triumphant close of his twenty-three-year quest can never be his."

Peary's Early Life and Education

Peary's life was divided into two parts — preparation and accomplishment. From earliest boyhood he fought for everything he had, or did. There was no golden spoon, or even a silver one, in his mouth when he entered the world, May 6, 1856, in the little town of Cresson, Pennsylvania. His father and uncles made "shooks" — staves for the manufacture of barrels. It wasn't a lucrative business. The first blow came when Peary was three years old. His father died. His mother took her husband's body and her little son to her native state of Maine, at South Portland. Peary lived until after college in that rugged state.

He loved nature passionately. He taught himself taxidermy and added materially to the resources of the family by mounting birds and animals. One of his dominating characteristics, according to Hobbs, was a complete indifference to personal comfort. One day while hunting near Fryeburg, Maine, a friend killed two ducks in the middle of a frozen pond. He was going to leave them, but Robert pulled off his clothes, broke the ice in front of him with a fence rail, and swam out to retrieve the birds. He was an all-around athlete, an expert shot, a fine horseman and particularly good in all winter sports. He thought nothing of walking twenty-five miles in seven or eight hours and did it every week.

After high school Peary entered Bowdoin College in Brunswick, having won in competition the Brown Memorial Scholarship. He chose civil engineering as his major course. When twenty years old he graduated from Bowdoin second in his class, with top honors in engineering, and was elected to Phi Beta Kappa. Then he became for a time town surveyor of Fryeburg and did a year or two as draftsman in the Coast and Geodetic Survey at Washington. Peary apparently enjoyed his job, but the virus of exploration was working in his blood. He thought of Panama. Talk of a canal was in the air, and he projected a plan to explore the Isthmus, combining natural history with engineering studies. But his mother turned thumbs down on the expedition, and he took the examination for the Civil Engineering Corps of the U.S. Navy. Out of two hundred contestants, only four passed the grueling technical and physical requirements. Peary was one of the four. His first job was work on a naval pier at Key West, Florida, under the distinguished engineer A. G. Menocal. A method of sinking the iron plates for the pier devised by Peary saved the government $24,000 and gained Menocal's admiration. By a strange trick of fate, Peary's next assignment took him to the Isthmus, the very place he had been hoping to explore.

Upon the organization of the Provincial Interoceanic Canal Society in 1880, the U.S. government offered to the society the services of naval engineers and put Menocal in charge. He chose Peary as his chief assistant. Even then, when he was twenty-eight years old and en route to the tropics, he may have begun to dream of the conquest of the North Pole.

Surveying for a Nicaraguan Canal

Writing in his diary of "San Salvador, the land which first gladdened the eyes of Columbus," he said: "Birthplace of the new world, purple against the yellow sunset, as it was almost four hundred years ago when it smiled a welcome to the man whose fame can be equalled only by him who shall one day stand with 360 degrees of longitude beneath his motionless feet and for whom East and West shall have vanished — the discoverer of the North Pole."

The Nicaraguan job proved to be a tough assignment. Peary, as pioneer and transit man, had to cut his way with a band of *macheteros* through an almost impenetrable jungle. Often, the men waded in slush and mud, waist deep on a quaking bottom, and plunged into holes over their heads. Before the survey could be finished, their leave from the Navy Department had almost expired. Working against time, Peary did a Herculean job in completing the task. Menocal was almost lyrical in his praise of Peary. The phrases "untiring energy," "tremendous endurance," "devotion to duty," "absolute integrity" run through the official reports on Peary's work which Menocal sent to the Navy Department.

[14   ]

With the building of the canal in prospect, it seemed inevitable that Peary's next years would be spent in the tropics, but I have always believed that an explorer's ultimate destiny is determined by hereditary biological factors which will not be denied. They eventually triumph over environment or circumstance, leading him to the path he was born to follow. Peary was a pure Nordic, tall and spare, with a powerful body, blue eyes and light hair. One could easily picture him standing on the bow of a Viking ship, sailing into uncharted seas to discover what lay beyond the ocean's rim — but not cutting his way through steaming tropical jungles. That is for the Mediterranean type, not the Nordic! Thus, one evening he was browsing in an old book store in Washington, where, he writes, "I came upon a fugitive paper on the Inland Ice of Greenland. A chord, which as a boy had vibrated intensely in me at the reading of Kane's wonderful book, was touched again. I read all I could upon the subject, noted the conflicting experiences of Nordenskjöld, Jensen, and the rest and felt that I must see for myself what the truth was of this mysterious interior."

Sixty-six years ago, the Arctic regions were largely *terra incognita*. No one knew whether or not Greenland was an island; or that it did not extend to, and beyond, the North Pole. Greenland had never been crossed. The few explorers who had penetrated its interior had found a thick ice cap, deep crevasses, and slopes rising to several thousand feet. Even during the summer, fierce blizzards swept across this glacier mass. Peary determined to be the first man to traverse Greenland from one coast to the other.

First Greenland Expedition

He seems to have had no difficulty in obtaining leave from the Navy Department, and his mother loaned him five hundred dollars to finance the expedition. The whaler *Eagle*, Captain Jackman, Master, dropped the amateur Arctic explorer off at Disco Island, June 6, 1886. Eventually he got a skin boat to take him to the mainland where he engaged Christian Maigaard, the assistant manager of a little settlement of Eskimos, for the ice journey.

Pulling two sledges up the face of the glacier to the top was hard work, but after two days they reached the landward edge of the ice cap at an elevation of 1956 feet. East from this camp stretched an ice plain, cut by deep cracks and crevasses, usually marked by snow bridges. One bridge broke through, and Peary just managed to hang by his arms and scramble out. He was pretty well shaken as he looked down at the ragged blue walls, festooned with giant icicles and frostwork of fantastic patterns, lost in the blue-black night of the unknown depths. Day after day the men pushed on until, at 7525 feet elevation, a southeasterly gale developed and for two days and nights they lay under a rubber blanket with the wind and snow driving in an incessant, sullen roar across the drift above them. On July 19th, the gale ceased and Peary got a good observation of the sun. This camp was almost one hundred miles from the margin of the ice cap. From there they turned back because of lack of food.

The results of Peary's initial attempt at Arctic exploration were unspectacular, but he had penetrated inland farther than any other explorer and had reached a greater elevation. Most important of all, however, was what he had learned of the characteristics of the ice cap and of Arctic travel and equipment. Moreover, his feet were now set on the path that eventually led him to the North Pole.

Back in Washington, a perverse fate still tried to push him southward into the tropics. A new organization, the Maritime Canal Company of Nicaragua, decided upon a final survey of the route. Menocal was again in charge, with Peary second in command.

Matthew Henson, his Negro body servant, accompanied Peary on this expedition. The faithful man never left him, and finally stood at his side when he raised the American flag at the North Pole. "Mat" is still alive, well into his eighties. He worships Peary, almost as a god.

The canal survey was completed in 1888 when Peary was thirty-two years old. At this time he married in Washington Josephine Diebitsch, daughter of a professor in the Smithsonian Institution. It could not have been a happier union. All their lives the couple were devoted and their home life was ideal. But it was a hard role for a young wife. She knew that her husband was dedicated to exploration and that it would mean hardship and long separation, but she always gave Peary fullest support in his ambitions.

A little more than a month after the wedding, news came that Nansen had made the first crossing of Greenland. This was a great disappointment to Peary, but he projected a new plan. He would explore the ice cap in a general north-easterly direction and would find out whether or not Greenland was an island and if it led to the Pole.

[17   ]

Second Greenland Expedition

He set about raising the money, and in 1891 ten thousand
dollars had been subscribed. The expedition sailed June 6,
1891, on the sealer *Kite*, and included Mrs. Peary and six
others, among whom was Dr. Frederick A. Cook, surgeon.
Also there was a group of scientists from Philadelphia. It
was Cook's first trip to the North. Mrs. Peary became the
first white woman to spend a winter in the Arctic.

In Melville Bay, the *Kite* ran into heavy ice floes. Peary
was leaning over the stern rail when a great ice cake hit the
rudder. One of the spokes of the wheel caught Peary's leg
and snapped both bones just above the ankle. Dr. Cook set
the fractures. The others wanted Peary to return to the
U.S. on the *Kite* but he would not consider such a course,
and when the ship reached the party's winter quarters in
Inglefield Gulf, he was carried ashore. It was five weeks before he could walk, but he directed the work of building the
house and never complained at his hard luck. The camp was
named Red Cliff House.

Before the long night set in, it was imperative to obtain
the winter's supply of meat. Peary, Dr. Cook, Mrs. Peary,
Mat Henson, and two Eskimos were in a small boat when
they discovered a herd of walrus on an ice pan, and
harpooned a big female. She gave them a regular "Nantucket
sleigh ride" before they put a bullet in her head. Peary
writes: "Our appetite for sport had been only whetted by
this adventure and we had a new and still more exciting experience a few minutes later. We suddenly ran into a school
and blazing away we killed two of the animals. The rest of
them resented our intrusion, and we suddenly became the

hunted instead of the hunters. There were perhaps one hundred of the enraged brutes and we had the hardest kind of work to keep them away from the boat. Our repeaters blazed continuously, and to add to the din, Ikwa beat a lively tattoo on the boat with his harpoon and emitted the most startling yells. Mrs. Peary was very cool through it all, and slipping down from her seat beside me in the stern into the bottom of the boat, where she could with her body shield my injured leg, now knitting in the splints, from the excited movements of the others, she steadily filled the magazines of our Winchesters as they were emptied and enabled us to keep up such a continuous fire that the huge brutes, though fiercely and repeatedly led to the charge by an old bull, could not stand the uninterrupted blaze and crash of our repeaters."

By the time the sun left, they had collected 11 walrus, 41 reindeer (caribou), 4 seals, 1 bear, and 300 little auks and guillemots. These birds are a great source of food to the Eskimos as well as to every Arctic explorer. George Borup, who was on Peary's successful polar expedition of 1909, says of them: "On the top of the mountain we saw a couple of the implements [nets] the Eskimos use to catch little auks. All you have to do is to sit down on the rocks, it being immaterial whether you are out of sight or not. The auks, returning from the sea where they've been feeding, fly in countless thousands — one big stream. It is impossible to convey any idea, no matter what one may say, of their incredible numbers. . . . They don't fly high and all you have to do is to make wild swings and you will surely catch something. . . . They are about as big as robins. . . . Harry Whitney tells of a huskie [Eskimo] who bagged —

or netted — two hundred and eighty in three hours. The natives supplied Dr. Kane with eight thousand per week. Langdon Gibson [brother of Charles Dana Gibson] who was with the Commander in '91, got ninety odd, I think, in one shoot."

Discovery of Independence Bay

For the trip across the ice cap, Peary chose only Astrup, a young Danish ski expert, as a companion, for he believed that a small party could be more effective than a larger one. Gibson and Cook accompanied them for the first 130 miles to help with the loads, and then returned. The explorers set out May 3rd, with three sleds, and fourteen dogs, and laid their course northeastward, traveling at night to avoid the glare of the sun. Long marches over hard snow stretches, halts for blizzards and detours for crevasses and ponds on the ice surface, formed the order of their days. At times the men suffered from heat in their fur clothes. Land was sighted on June 26th, and five days later a wide trenchlike opening with cliffs on either side could be clearly seen. The descent from the ice cap was abrupt, and streams of thaw-water had to be forded every few miles. They had tough going over a great moraine dotted with patches of snow. The jagged rocks cut their foot gear so badly that both men had to use mittens, caps, and parts of clothing to keep their feet covered. Here Peary killed his first musk ox: "Two were lying down, less than a hundred yards away. One was entirely quiet but the other turned his head in my direction as I coughed in my excitement. My crippled leg had thrown me out of all the deer [reindeer] hunts about Red Cliff, and lack of practice and the nature of the game before me gave me the severest kind of buck fever. As I raised my Winchester it was with the utmost difficulty that I could keep the sight on that great shaggy head. I pulled the trigger and heard the bullet reach the mark somewhere. Much to my surprise, as I appeared on the scene he rose leisurely and advanced toward me, as if to see what might be the trouble. A second shot point blank staggered and discouraged him, and he turned away giving me the desired shot back of the fore shoulder. As he fell, the other rose leisurely, exposing as he did so, the same fatal shot . . .

"Familiar with descriptions and pictures of the musk ox, I had yet obtained no true conceptions of the appearance of these strange denizens of the fartherest north . . . they were just shedding their heavy winter coats of wool and this, as it worked out through the long coarse black hair of the summer coat, fell to the ground on either side, giving the animal the appearance of size greatly in excess of the reality. This, with their slow sedate movements, made an impression which I shall never forget."

Twenty-six miles from the moraine they climbed a long incline to a plateau which fell away in a sheer wall 3800 feet high. Below them lay a great bay of the sea. Peary writes: "Before us stretched new lands and waters, to which, with the explorer's prerogative, I gave names. . . . It was almost impossible for us to believe that we were standing on the northern shore of Greenland as we gazed from the summit of this bronze cliff with the most brilliant sunshine all about us, with yellow poppies growing between the rocks around our feet, and a herd of musk oxen in the valley behind us."

Peary named the fiord Independence Bay in honor of the day, July 4th. At the summit of what he called Navy Cliff, he erected a cairn of stones and in it placed an outline of his crossing, "Which should be in the coming years the silent record of our visit here." In 1912, more than twenty years after Peary's discovery, the Danish North Greenland Expedition under the famous explorer Knud Rasmussen recovered the record, which read:

Have this day, with one companion, Eivind Astrup, and eight dogs, reached this point via the Inland Ice from McCormick Bay, Whale Sound. We have travelled over 500 miles, and both we and the dogs are in good condition. I have named this Fiord "Independence" in honor of that day, July 4th, dear to all Americans, on which we looked down into it.

Have killed five musk oxen in the valley above and seen several others. I start back for Whale Sound tomorrow.

R. E. Peary, U.S. Navy

Of this discovery Dr. Hobbs says: "There were also two American papers. To this precious record Peter Freuchen added (in Danish) 'Taken from the cairn on Navy Cliff the 22nd of July 1912, and handed over to Knud Rasmussen, the Leader of the Expedition.' Freuchen also reported that the tracks in the gravel of Peary and his companion, as they had leaned against the cairn, were well preserved after a score of years."

The return journey, when they had regained the interior ice cap, was a dreary succession of blizzards, fog, and high winds. Several of the dogs gave out and had to be fed to the living animals. On August 3rd, after three months on the ice cap, the familiar land near Red Cliff base came into view. They had covered 1200 miles on the round trip. "This first great sledge journey of Peary's in north Greenland had almost completely realized his expectations through discovering the sea on the east coast and making probable, though it did not prove, the insularity of the great land mass," says Dr. Hobbs.

Third Greenland Expedition

Upon his return to the United States, Peary was acclaimed as a hero of Arctic exploration. In later years, he often told me, "The time to prepare for your next expedition is when you have just returned from a successful trip." Thus, no sooner had he reached civilization than he launched a bigger program for Greenland exploration. He hoped to set out with a sledge party of eight men, and upon arriving at Independence Bay, divide it into three groups for exploring both to the north and the south.

It was a much too ambitious project and later he admitted that he had made the fatal mistake of taking too large a party.

He had some difficulty with the navy, even though he had brought honor to the service, but eventually he was granted a three-year leave. A large part of the finances were obtained through a very successful lecture tour when, in a hundred days, he delivered 165 lectures.

The *Falcon*, Captain Harry Bartlett (brother of Bob), Master, was chartered to take the party north and sailed from Philadelphia on June 26, 1893. The fourteen members of the expedition again included Mrs. Peary, who was expecting a child, and a nurse, Mrs. Susan J. Cross.

At Bowdoin Bay, on Inglefield Gulf, Greenland, they built a house named Anniversary Lodge. The *Falcon* sailed for home August 20th. On September 12th, Mrs. Peary gave birth to a baby girl, who was christened Marie Ahnighito Peary, after the great meteorite discovered on this expedition by Peary, and came to be known as the "Snow Baby."

The expedition, which began so auspiciously, did not achieve the spectacular results for which Peary had hoped. Several of the men became ill, or were not fitted to endure the hardships of the inland ice. At the end of three years he had made another crossing of Greenland, done minor explorations, and accumulated weather data which was of great scientific importance but had no popular appeal. The discovery of three of the world's greatest meteorites, however, did help to give the public what it wanted in the way of something to talk about.

Discovering the World's Greatest Meteorites

A secondary object of the 1894 expedition was to find the mysterious "iron mountain" of the Smith Sound Eskimos of which Captain John Ross had heard in his Arctic expedition of 1818. Ross found that the Eskimos had knives and harpoon points with cutting edges of iron. He thought these might come from a meteorite. The natives depended entirely upon this source for their metal, and for three quarters of a century had refused to tell later British and Danish explorers where it was located. But Peary was different. He had proved himself their friend and given them knives and guns, spears, needles, and other things that literally changed their lives. By unanimous consent of the little tribe, they agreed to guide him to the place where they obtained their iron. It was, they said, on the northern shore of Melville Bay, east of Cape York, Greenland. In May of 1894, with a companion, Hugh J. Lee, and one Eskimo, Peary started on a journey which proved to be one of the most difficult and dangerous of his entire career. They were delayed day after day by terrific storms, and had to cross the mouth of Granville Bay by leaping from one cake of broken ice to another. At the end of a smaller inlet near the southern slope of a mountain, he found the meteorites — three of them — where they had hurtled out of the sky at some time in the far, dim past.

One, the Eskimos called the "Woman," for to them it resembled a woman sewing; the other was named the "Dog." But six miles away lay the great one, "Ahnighito," the "Tent." According to their superstition, an Inniut woman and her dog and tent were thrown out of Heaven by Tonarsuk, the Spirit of Evil. The two smaller ones rested upon the rocks, but the Tent was nearly buried in the earth on a terrace eighty feet above high-water mark and a hundred yards from shore. Peary recognized that the Tent was by far the largest known meteorite in the world, and that the three were of paramount value to science. To bring them to New York was a "must," but he knew it would be a difficult job.

Of the return journey, Lee writes: "We went nearly, or perhaps more than, 200 miles in four days, with nothing to eat, dragging the sledges through very deep snow, and were compelled by open water to climb glaciers from 1000 to 3000 feet high, and on one occasion we had to cut steps or footholds in the icy surface for several hundred feet, and then carry sledges, loads, and dogs up on our backs." Actually the men averaged about 65 miles per march, a near record. They returned to Anniversary Lodge on June 6th.

Later Peary made two unsuccessful attempts to revisit the meteorites, but heavy ice and storms in Melville Bay defeated him both times. It was not until 1895 that his relief steamer *Kite* pushed into the estuary within a mile and a half of where the celestial visitors lay in their bleak surroundings. The Woman weighed 5500 pounds, and the Dog 1000 pounds. Ahnighito, Peary thought, was as much as 100 tons but it has never been actually weighed. Estimates put it at 65 tons. By the use of jacks, the two smaller masses of iron were hoisted onto a sledge of spruce poles and dragged to the water's edge. But the Woman was nearly lost after all their work. She was placed on a huge cake of ice, forty feet by twenty and seven feet thick, and ferried to the ship. Just as the *Kite's* tackles were made fast to hoist her aboard, the ice cake split. But the lines held, new ones were warped about the sullen lady, although she was half submerged, and she was hoisted over the ship's side. The Tent could not be dislodged from its age-long bed. Two ten-ton screw-jacks crumpled without moving the giant. The *Kite* had to retreat to escape being frozen in for the winter.

Attempts to Remove the Tent

The next year, 1896, Peary went north with a larger ship, the *Hope*, of 307 tons net register, and with more powerful appliances. What happened can best be told in his own words: "The first thing to be done was to tear the heavenly visitor from its frozen bed of centuries and, as it rose slowly, inch by inch under the resistless heft of the hydraulic jacks, gradually displaying its ponderous sides, it grew upon us as Niagara grows upon the observer, and there was not one of us unimpressed by the enormousness of this lump of metal. The expressions of the Eskimos about the *saviksoah* (the great iron) were low but earnest and it, and the other great irons (the jacks) which could tear it from its bed, awed them to the utmost . . . It was interesting and irritating, to watch the stubbornness of the monster as it sulked and hung back to the last inch . . . Urged by the resistless lift of the jacks, the huge brown mass would slowly and stubbornly rise on its side, and be forced to a position of unstable equilibrium . . . When it struck the ground, the harder rocks would elicit streams of sparks from its brown surface before they crumbled, the softer ones would dissolve into dust and smoke, and the giant would bury itself half its depth in the earth, with the slow resistless motion of a hydraulic punch cutting cold iron, then lunge suddenly forward a few feet, throwing up a dam of earth and stones before it like the terminal moraine of a glacier . . . Never have I had the terrific majesty of the force of gravity and the meaning of the terms 'momentum' and 'inertia' so powerfully brought home to me, as in handling this mountain of iron . . .

"When lowered slowly upon heavy timber-blocking by the jacks, it settled resistlessly into the wood until it seemed as if it would never stop . . . it would bite into the steel rails like a punch and the rail itself would sink into the timber beneath if near the middle, or crush through it if near the end."

The sixty-ton jack gave out and the weight damaged the thirty-ton jacks that had done most of the work. Progress became so slow that before he could get the meteorite close to the shore, the pack ice of Melville Bay, driving in upon the beach, forced him to pull the ship out with haste to avoid having her crushed like an eggshell against the rocks.

Peary was bitterly disappointed, but his determination to bring the great mass of iron to New York and the American Museum of Natural History was only strengthened. The word "failure" simply did not exist in his vocabulary. The next year, 1897, he again went north in the *Hope*, with stronger planks, heavier rails, and more powerful jacks. Foot by foot the monster was dragged from land across a bridge to the ship, and lowered onto a bed of great oak timbers in the hold. Hurriedly the explorers braced it, for bad weather was in the offing. Out across Davis Strait they steamed, into the teeth of a furious storm. The superstitious sailors of the *Hope* thought their last hour had come, for they were sure the iron had supernatural powers and the Devil himself would prevent it from ever leaving its northern home. Of this experience Peary writes: ". . . during the night of Sept. 8th, the *Hope* rolled and pitched dizzily upon the furious seas till the grey light of dawn began to filter through the tumult. Time after time the lee dead-eyes were under water, and as the *Hope* leaned and wavered and hesitated with her rail out of sight, and the boiling tumult to leeward seething up to the side of the companionway, it seemed as if she would never right . . .

"Crouched behind the weather rail, with eyes just pupil-width above it, I watched the turmoil. The wind, resistless and sonorous as Niagara, roared across the seething waters, almost as tangible as they . . . More than one anxious heart on board was certain at every wave shock that the demoniac iron had broken loose and was smashing a way for itself through the ship's side, and more than one gave up hope of ever seeing the morning light again."

But the bracing held. Next morning they steamed under the lee of Cape of God's Mercy, named by Davis centuries ago. Every man on board offered thanks to the One who gives life and takes it away.

Bringing the great meteorite to New York was a high spot in Peary's career. The difficulties had seemed almost insurmountable, and had he not been an engineer of unusual ability and a man who refused to fail, it never could have been accomplished.

Today, all three of the Cape York meteorites are on exhibition in the Hayden Planetarium of the American Museum of Natural History, in New York City. Thousands of visitors pass by Ahnighito every year, but few of them know that, for centuries, it was sacred to the Eskimos; few know of the heartbreaking toil, and the near tragedy, that marked its journey from the bleak shores of Greenland to its present home.

The North Pole Becomes the Goal of Peary's Life

Back in America, Peary had definitely decided to make the North Pole the goal of his life. In 1898, when in London to receive the Patrons' Gold Medal of the Royal Geographic Society, he announced his plans, which had already been outlined to the American Geographic Society. He wanted an especially strong ship that could push through the ice into the Arctic Ocean, where he intended to locate an advanced base. Lord Northcliffe, publisher of the *Daily Mail*, became interested in Peary and offered him the *Windward*, which was to be re-engined for the expedition.

Morris K. Jesup was not only president of the American Museum of Natural History, but of the American Geographic Society as well, and he, with other prominent men, undertook to assist in financing the expedition. But immediately difficulty was encountered from the navy. In Europe and England, the great Arctic explorers had been mostly naval men and their respective services looked upon their work with national pride. Not so the American Navy. Its officers envied Peary's continual leaves, and failed to recognize either his splendid courage or his amazing achievements in the face of incredible obstacles. Peary's request for leave to attempt to reach the Pole met with a flat refusal, in spite of letters from Mr. Jesup and other eminent men and scientific institutions. He was ordered to report to the commandant of the naval station at Mare Island, California, "for such duty as he may assign."

But fortunately, Mr. Charles A. Moore, a Republican businessman who had helped McKinley attain the Presidency of the United States, solved the difficulty by going directly to the President on Peary's behalf.

Under Mr. Jesup's stimulation, and that of Herbert L. Bridgeman, twenty-five men had pledged $100,000 during the four-year period of the expedition. But the war with Spain broke out, and only eight fulfilled their promises. In addition, the *Windward* could not be re-engined, due to a mechanics' strike in England. As she was, she had nowhere near enough power to buck the ice. Then, a Norwegian expedition, under the command of the veteran Arctic explorer Sverdrup, announced that it was to start at the same time from the same region with the Pole as its goal. Moreover, Sverdrup would have Nansen's famous ship, the *Fram*.

Since Peary's plans had been announced far in advance, this was contrary to the best traditions of exploration, and might produce all sorts of complications in the discovery and naming of new lands. Peary could not wait for the slow *Windward* if he were not to lose out entirely, and so went north in the *Hope*, which the Peary Arctic Club now provided for the purpose. The *Windward* followed at her own speed.

Sverdrup was unable to force the *Fram* into the ice-jammed Kennedy Channel, and did not attempt to reach the Pole. Nevertheless, his field of exploration overlapped and caused dispute as to priority in the discovery and naming of a large land area. Peary never forgave Sverdrup. It was the latter's endorsement of Dr. Cook which played so large a part in Cook's temporary acclaim at Copenhagen as the discoverer of the North Pole.

Peary, too, found the ice impassable, and the weakengined *Windward* was imprisoned in Kane Basin, far to the south. Thus, he would have to track his supplies four hundred miles before commencing his dash for the Pole, which was another four hundred miles away across the sea ice. He landed his equipment at Cape D'Urville, and decided to transport it to Fort Conger, the base which Greely had abandoned fifteen years earlier.

While waiting for the ice to be in condition for sledging, Peary explored and mapped the unknown region to the west of Kane Basin. Here he met Sverdrup, and while the two great explorers shook hands, their greeting was cold. During this exploration, Peary demonstrated that Greely's "Schley Land" and "Hayes Sound" were nonexistent.

Night Sledging

In the early winter of 1898, Peary began sledging his equipment to Fort Conger. He did not believe that he could reach the Pole, starting from such a great distance to the south, but he determined to do his best on behalf of his sponsors. Establishing a chain of caches, he worked all during the Arctic night, whenever there was moonlight, relaying his supplies northward.

"No one," writes Peary, "who has not had the actual experience, can imagine the work and annoyance involved in transporting in semi- or complete darkness, these supplies along the frightful ice-foot which everywhere lines the ragged Grinnell Land waste." December was intensely cold, and very nearly ended Peary's career as an explorer. "The light of the moon lasted for only a few hours out of twenty-four," he says, "and at its best was not sufficient to permit us to select a route on the sea ice . . . Just south of Cape Defosse we ate the last of our biscuit; just north of it, the last of our beans . . .

"The moon had left us entirely now, and the ice-foot was utterly impracticable, and we groped and stumbled through the rugged sea ice as far as Cape Baird. Here we slept for a few hours in a burrow in the snow, then started across Lady Franklin Bay. In complete darkness, and over a chaos of broken and heaved-up ice, we stumbled and fell and groped for eighteen hours, till we climbed upon the ice-foot of the north side. Here a dog was killed for food.

"Absence of suitable snow put an igloo out of the question, and a semi-cave under a large cake of ice was so cold that we could stop only long enough to make tea. Here I left a broken sledge and nine exhausted dogs. Just east of us a floe had been driven ashore, and forced up over the ice-foot till its shattered fragments lay a hundred feet up the talus of the bluff. It seemed impassable, but the crack at the edge of the ice foot allowed us to squeeze through; and soon after we rounded the point, and I was satisfied by the 'feel' of the shore, for we could see nothing, that we were at one of the entrances of Discovery Harbour, but which, I could not tell.

"Several hours of groping showed that it was the eastern entrance. We had struck Bellot Island, and at midnight of January 6th, we were stumbling through the dilapidated door of Fort Conger.

"A little remaining oil enabled me by the light of our sledge cooker, to find the range and the stove in the officers' quarters and, after some difficulty, fires were started in both. When this was accomplished a suspicious 'wooden' feeling in the right foot led me to have my *kamiks* pulled off, and I found, to my annoyance, that both feet were frosted.

". . . it was evident that I should lose parts or all of several toes, and be confined for some weeks. The minimum mean temperature during the trip was −51.9°F., the lowest −63°F."

Peary wrote that the interior of the Greely camp, which had been abandoned fifteen years before, was ". . . a scene of the utmost confusion. The floors of the officers' and men's rooms, kitchen, and vestibule were littered and blocked with boxes, empty and packed, trunks, cast-off clothing and rubbish of various descriptions. In the kitchen, cans containing remnants of tea, coffee, etc. were scattered about, with the rest of what had been their contents spilled on the floor and table. In the men's room, dishes remained on tables just as left after lunch or dinner on the day when the fort was deserted. Biscuits scattered in every direction, overturned cups, etc. gave indications of a hasty departure."

Most of the great quantity of supplies had spoiled, and the delicate scientific instruments and specimens were ruined beyond recovery. They had been left in a lean-to instead of being stored in the house, where they would have been safe.

It is not surprising that Greely should have bitterly resented it when Peary published this report. Greely had been enjoying the status of an Arctic hero. Instead he was shown to be an incompetent leader who was responsible for the death of most of his command at Starvation Camp, where they had fled in panic. Peary also demonstrated by his own sledging trips and discovery of game that the tragedy was completely unnecessary.

Fort Conger

For six dreary weeks, Peary lay in semi-darkness on his back in the dilapidated shelter at Fort Conger, suffering excruciating pain from his frozen feet. It seemed that all his hopes for attaining the Pole, or even being able to live, were ended, but his indomitable spirit would not let him give up. In his lowest moment he wrote on the wall his motto, "I shall find a way or make one."

When he could stand for a few minutes, he determined to return to the *Windward*, where his toes could be amputated, and the party set out in moonlight for the 250-mile journey along the broken ice foot. He wrote: "I remember few more grim and desolate scenes than the environs of Fort Conger as I took them in while being lashed to my sledge, a helpless cripple, on the bitterly cold February morning when I left the fort to return to the *Windward*. The dead-white slopes of the hills lifting to the lifeless blue-black sky, the dead white expanse of harbor and bay reaching away to the ribbon of pale, steely light past the black blot of Cape Leiber . . . are deeply graven on my memory. The un-relieved blackness of the preceding six weeks, during which I lay there on my back, accompany the scene as a nightmare."

On March 13th all but the little toes of both Peary's feet were amputated. Even before they had healed, he set out on a remarkable series of journeys to explore the land west of Kane Basin, which was then completely unknown. The

[35]

season was so far advanced toward summer that the ice, in places, was covered with pools through which the men had to wade, sometimes waist deep. It caused excruciating pain to Peary's maimed feet.

In the meantime, back in New York, a group of men under the leadership of Peary's devoted friend Morris K. Jesup had formally organized the Peary Arctic Club on January 29, 1899, and arranged to send a ship north each summer during his stay in the Arctic. The *Diana* arrived August 12th, at Etah, Greenland, whence the *Windward* had gone when released from the ice. Herbert Bridgeman, one of Peary's strongest backers, was on board and urged Peary to return because of his mutilated feet. He replied, "When my furlough has expired or I have reached the Pole, I shall be ready to go."

First Attempt to Reach the Pole, 1902

It was not until the spring of 1902 that he was able to make a serious assault on the Pole. Bad weather, and a long delay because of open water at what he called the "Big Lead" or "Grand Canal," prevented him from advancing farther than 84° 17′ 27″ N. over the sea ice. Nevertheless, this was a "fartherest north" for the Western Hemisphere.

On August 5th, the *Windward* arrived, with Mrs. Peary and Marie on board, to bring him home. He had spent four years in the Arctic. At this time, Dr. Fridtjof Nansen wrote of him: "I do not know what I admire most with Peary—the indefatigable energy with which he works for his goal, year after year, and in the teeth of the most formidable odds, or the never failing readiness with which he overcomes the greatest and most unexpected difficulties.

"By his long labors in the far north Commander Peary has been able to finally settle the northern extension of Greenland and thus has probably defined and mapped the most northern land of the earth. This was one of the greatest geographical problems of the North Polar region."

And yet Peary felt that he had failed. The question was, could any man succeed in reaching the Pole over the shifting ice? The British had long ago arrived at the conclusion that it was impossible. But Peary would not admit impossibility. He underwent an operation in Philadelphia on his feet. Dr. W. W. Keen removed the useless little toes, which projected beyond the stumps of the others; then he slit the skin at the front of the feet, drew forward the tissue from underneath and behind the toes to make a cushion for the stumps. With these makeshift feet, Peary carried on all his remaining exploration.

His previous experience convinced him that it was essential to have a ship which could force its way through the ice of the narrow Kennedy and Robeson Channels into the Arctic Ocean itself. Thus he could make his dash for the Pole from the nearest point of land, without the handicap of starting from a base far to the south. If he had had such a vessel, his last sledge journey would, in distance, have carried him far beyond the Pole.

But no such ship existed. Nansen's *Fram* was so built that ice pressure would squeeze the hull above the level of compression. But the *Fram's* engines were nowhere near strong enough to break the ice. She could drift, but not force her way through the pack. He needed $100,000; Morris K. Jesup and Thomas H. Hubbard, another supporter, pledged

$50,000 each if the Peary Arctic Club could raise another $50,000. This he was finally able to do, and Judge Darling, assistant secretary of the navy, agreed that the expedition would be sponsored by the navy, but without any financial support. It was the only recognition of his work the navy had given him ungrudgingly.

Peary himself designed the ship. The *Fram* was a sailing vessel with auxiliary power; Peary's craft was to be a steamer with auxiliary sails.

"When it came to finding a name," Peary wrote, "for the ship by whose aid I hoped to fight my way toward the most inaccessible spot on earth, the name of 'Roosevelt' seemed to be the one and inevitable name. It held up as an ideal . . . those very qualities of strength, insistence, persistence, and unvarying victory over all obstacles which made the twenty-sixth President of the United States so great."

The ship was launched March 23, 1905. She was 184 feet over-all, with a beam of 35½ feet and a draft load of 16 feet. Her sides were thirty inches thick, of strongest wood, heavily braced by struts, and steel-sheathed outside. She had a sharply raking stem that would rise on the ice at each blow. The detachable propeller blades and massive rudder could be drawn up when required.

Second Polar Attempt, on the Roosevelt

On July 16, 1905, the *Roosevelt* sailed north, with "Bob" Bartlett as captain. Peary took aboard fifty Eskimos and two hundred dogs; they made the ship a bedlam at all hours of the day and night. When the *Roosevelt* entered the pack ice surging down Smith Sound, Peary wrote: "In all my experience, I recall nothing more exciting than the thrill, the crash, the shock of hurling the *Roosevelt*, a fifteen-hundred-ton battering ram, at the ice to smash a way through, or the tension of the moments when, caught in the resistless grip of two great ice fields, I have stood on the bridge and seen the deck amidships slowly bulge upward, and the rigging slacken with the compression of the sides . . .

"Again, I can see Bartlett up in the crow's nest, at the head of the swaying mast, jumping up and down like a madman, swearing, shouting to the ship, exhorting it like a coach with his man in the ring."

The battle of the ship against the ice, as she forced her way through Kennedy and Robeson Channels, is an epic of polar history. She did not escape undamaged. Once, a sudden swirl of the current smashed her against the ice foot and ground her, bumping hard, along its face. In a few minutes the back of the rudder had been twisted and the steel tiller rods snapped. But she got away before the ice caught her, and lay up at Cape Brevoort for five days while the damage was repaired. Her supreme test came in crossing to the west side of Robeson Channel, not far from the entrance to the Arctic Ocean. Peary was a writer of great ability, and I cannot resist quoting another passage from his description of the ship which he had conceived and built. He says: "The *Roosevelt* fought like a gladiator, turning, twisting, straining with all her force, smashing her full weight against the heavy floes whenever we could get room for a rush, and rearing upon them like a steeple-chaser taking a fence.

[39]

Ah, the thrill and tension of it, the lust of battle, which crowded days of ordinary life into one.

"The forward rush, the gathering speed and momentum, the crash, the upward heave, the grating snarl of the ice as the steel-shod stem split it as a mason's hammer splits granite, or trod it under, or sent it right and left in whirling fragments, followed by the violent roll, the backward rebound, and then the gathering for another rush, were glorious . . .

"At such times everyone on deck hung with breathless interest on our movements, and as Bartlett and I clung in the rigging I heard him whisper through clenched teeth . . . 'Give it to 'em, Teddy! Give it to 'em!'"

At the end, when they had crossed to the Grinnell Land coast, and were resting in a pool of open water in Wrangel Bay, Peary wrote: ". . . the battle has been won by sheer brute insistence and I do not believe there is another ship afloat that would have survived the ordeal.

"Bartlett and I went to our rooms, worn with the long tension, and I fell asleep instantly."

In Winter Quarters at Cape Sheridan

After several more perilous days, the *Roosevelt* won through to the Arctic Ocean and was berthed in a niche in the ice foot at Cape Sheridan, but not in a safe position. It was the best they could do, for heavy floes lined the shore. Hunting parties were sent out to the inland Lake Hazen district and returned with musk oxen, caribou, hares, and salmon trout. Peary says: "The char (?) of North

Grant Land is a beautiful mottled fish, weighing sometimes as much as eleven or twelve pounds . . . I would spear one of these beauties and throw him on the ice to freeze, then pick him up and throw him down so as to shatter the flesh under the skin, lay him on the sledge, and as I walked away pick out morsels of the pink flesh and eat them as one would eat strawberries." The caribou was a new species which Peary had discovered in Ellesmere Land in 1902. It is a beautiful animal, snow white except for a small saddle of light brown. Dr. J. A. Allen named it *Rangifer pearyi*. The brown patch is so inconspicuous that Captain Bartlett, who had killed hundreds, would not believe it was anything but pure white until I showed him skins in the museum. I won a five-dollar bet from Bob.

On March 6th, the dash for the Pole began, with supporting parties leaving caches of food and alcohol and then returning to the main base. The temperature was low — from fifty to sixty-two below zero — but the sun was gradually creeping up so as to make a complete circuit of the horizon. The men were beset by unprecedented storms, which drove the ice eastward, and at the "Big Lead" were held up for six days before they could cross on young ice that swayed and undulated under their weight. The supporting-party system, which was designed to give food for the return, was completely disrupted by the strong internal movement of the ice pack that continually opened leads and threw up almost impassable barriers; some were hundreds of feet in height. Peary decided upon a Polar dash with Henson, in spite of insufficient supplies. Forced marches with little sleep and acute danger from opening ice, took them to 87° 6' N. — the "fartherest north" reached by any human being. That was a poor substitute for the Pole, but it had to do. There was no possibility of going farther with any chance of a safe return. It was with a heavy heart that Peary set his face toward Greenland. His observations showed that the unusual eastward drift of the ice made that coast the nearest land.

Return from Man's "Fartherest North"

The return journey was a race for life. An indescribable chaos of broken and rafted ice, open water, blizzards, and starvation put the last possible strain on their exhausted bodies as they forced their way southward. Peary was almost blind from the strain of taking continual observations in the dazzling light. The pain in his eyes was terrible. Time after time he buried his face in the snow until the eyelids were numb, to ease the ache. At the "Big Lead" they waited for five days for the water to freeze. On the fifth day, an Eskimo reported young ice in formation. In breathless silence, with feet wide apart, they crossed in safety, but as they were unfastening their snowshoes, the bridge of thin ice behind them parted again, and the lead began to widen. During the next three marches the desperate men hewed and hacked their way through a hell of heaped-up ice such as none of them had ever seen. Peary's mutilated feet caught it unmercifully, and he said that at their first camp his jaws ached from grinding his teeth together in the searing pain.

When they reached the northern shore of Greenland at Cape Neumeyer, they were almost dead from starvation.

Four hares helped to keep them going but, unless they found game soon, they were doomed men. Seven musk oxen saved their lives. Peary has given a graphic description of what it means to be hungry. He says: "The hunger that I do mean is that which has gone to the utmost limit consistent with the full retention of all the faculties, mental and physical . . . Now, as we lay there, looking at the big black animals before us we had none of the sportsmen's sensations in the presence of big game. They were not game for us, but meat! and every fibre in our gaunt bodies was vibrating with a savage lust for that meat — meat that should be soft and warm, meat into which our teeth could sink and tear and rend, meat that would not blister lips and tongue with its frost, nor ring like rock against our teeth . . .

"I can scarcely realize as I write these lines, what absolute animals hunger makes of men, and yet I can say truthfully, never have I tasted more delicious food than was that tender, raw, warm meat — a mouthful here, and a mouthful there, cut from the animal as I skinned it. I ate 'till I dared eat no more, although still unsatisfied."

For two days the men ate and slept without ceasing before continuing their way across Robeson Channel to Cape Sheridan and the *Roosevelt*. It was the one of the most remarkable marches ever made by an Arctic explorer. Of the 120 dogs that started, only 41 returned. The others had been fed to the living animals or eaten by the men. The unusual weather, and the strong eastward drift of the ice, had kept Peary from reaching the Pole but had not dimmed his determination to try again.

Exploring the Grant Land Coast

Before turning the ship southward for the homeward journey, he decided to explore 300 miles of unknown Grant Land coast to connect with Sverdrup's surveys to the west. Starting late in the season, with legs swollen from the effects of starvation and far below his normal strength, he accomplished his object but only with terrific suffering. The ice was covered with thaw-water which formed lakes and rivers. At times the men waded up to their armpits in the icy water while the dogs swam, the sledges kept afloat by inflated sealskins. Food they got by killing dogs, but the worst hardship was the constantly wet clothes. Peary's footgear began to disintegrate. He fitted his *kamiks* with tin soles from food cans. The stumps of his toes were in bad shape, aching and throbbing. By the time he reached the ship, Peary was almost finished. Bartlett says: "His foot gear was so saturated with water that it had long ceased to be of any use. He had on his feet pemmican tins and the inside ones were even reduced to the size of a Canadian nickel. Can you imagine a man with all his toes gone doing this? But he did."

There was bad news at the ship. The *Roosevelt* had broken out of her berth on July 4th, and had been smashed against the ice foot, breaking off her stern post and rudder as well as two blades from her propeller. "It was marvellous," Bartlett says, "the way Peary took the accident to the *Roosevelt*. He didn't turn a hair. It was this attitude in the face of privations and dangers that made us love and respect him." The next day Peary said to Bartlett, "We've got to get her back, Captain. We are going to come again next year." "I should have thought," Bartlett says, "he wouldn't have wanted ever to see that place again. But it was like him when he was lowest to be still planning for the future. Already he was thinking of his next attack on the Pole."

Getting the ship back to New York was an amazing performance of courage and seamanship. I have not space to give the details, but it is summed up by Rear Admiral Sigsbee, the hero of the *Maine:* "Peary's bringing of his ship, the *Roosevelt,* home in the late fall of 1906, fighting her through the heavy Arctic ice . . . encountering storm after storm, with rudder and stern post torn away, propeller crippled, and with pumps going constantly, has been characterized as one of the ablest, most resourceful and courageous affairs of its kind in the annals of Arctic exploration."

When Peary returned from this, his seventh expedition, he was more than fifty years of age. Twenty of those years had been spent in the Arctic or in preparations. At the half-century mark, a man has long passed his prime, and Peary knew all too well what a toll on his strength and endurance the last expedition had taken. Still, he had gained valuable knowledge of the sea ice. This he believed would outweigh his physical deterioration. He was more than ever convinced that his plan of supporting parties would work successfully, given normal weather conditions. On September 15, 1906, the President of the United States had written Morris K. Jesup:

> I think Peary is doing a good service to the whole nation, and I shall stand by him and see that he is not hurt by his absence.
> With kind regards, believe me,
> Faithfully yours,
Theodore Roosevelt

Roosevelt's faith, and that of Mr. Jesup, gave Peary re-
newed determination to try for the Pole again. He knew
it would be for the last time. Through the efforts of
Mr. Jesup, the Peary Arctic Club, and his own lectures,
sufficient money was raised to repair the *Roosevelt*, install
a new engine, and equip the expedition. Peary hoped to
get away by July 1, 1907, but work on the ship was not completed. Just at this time Mr. Jesup died. It was a crushing
blow, for not only was he a tower of strength financially,
but a devoted friend and a firm believer in Peary's ultimate
success. Peary wrote: "Yet when I gathered myself together
. . . I realized that the project was too big to die . . .
This feeling carried me past many a dead center of fatigue
and utter ignorance as to where the remaining money for
the expedition was to come from."

My First Meeting with Peary

It was in the early winter of 1906 that I met Peary for
the first time. I was newly come to the American Museum
of Natural History, a young man just out of college. For
years Peary had stood as my greatest hero. He was to lecture
at the museum in the evening, and I waited behind the huge
meteorite Ahnighito, then in the foyer, until he arrived.
He walked in alone. As he came opposite Ahnighito, he
paused for a moment and ran his hand over the surface of the
enormous mass of iron. A faraway look came into his eyes
and I knew he was seeing again the crashing waves and the
plunging ship battling for her life against the fury of the
sea, when he brought the meteorite from Greenland. Then
he went on to the president's office.

I hurried into the auditorium to a seat in the front row. Half an hour later, music sounded from somewhere in the Indian Hall, and Peary walked beside Morris K. Jesup, president of the museum, down the aisle and onto the platform. When he began to speak I seemed to go into another world — a world of snow and howling blizzards, of shifting ice and towering bergs. His story was simply told, with no heroics, but behind it one sensed the fatigue and suffering and hourly peril of that fruitless dash for the Pole. I felt, with him, the sickening disappointment when he knew that even though he had reached the "fartherest north" ever attained by man, he had failed again in the quest which he had almost strained his life out to achieve.

Next day I met him and shook his hand. He came with the director of the museum to the department of preparation, where I was working. Dr. Bumpus introduced me. I could hardly speak. To him, I was only an embarrassed young man; to me, he was the embodiment of all my youthful dreams.

A few months later I saw him again. For the next polar expedition an auxiliary ship, the *Erik*, was to go north to Etah, Greenland, with coal and additional supplies. The American Museum had received a considerable sum of money from Mr. George Bowdoin to provide an exhibition of water mammals. I had been studying whales, and the director asked Peary if he might send me on the *Erik* to collect seals, walrus, narwhale, and other porpoises. Peary said he would like to talk to me. Dr. Bumpus called me to his office and left us together. For a few moments I was tongue-tied, but he smiled and asked about my work on whales. He was keenly interested in natural history, he said, and had contributed largely to his college expenses by taxidermy, which he

[47]

taught himself. That put me at my ease, for I had done the same. At the end of half an hour, he said, yes, I could go on the *Erik,* and he would see that facilities were given for collecting, so far as possible.

I left treading on air, with the memory of his parting smile and warm handclasp. But my jubilation was short-lived. Not long after our conversation word came that the *Roosevelt* would not be ready until the following year, and the expedition must be postponed. In the meantime, I was sent to Alaska by the museum on a whaling cruise, and could not return until three months after the *Erik* sailed. I was bitterly disappointed at not being able to see Peary in the field, but on their return I came to know him and all the members of the expedition well, except Ross Marvin, who lost his life in the Arctic.

Bob Bartlett, Ross Marvin, Donald MacMillan, Dr. Goodsell, George Borup, Mat Henson! They were a wonderful group, hand-picked, each for some special qualification that would help put the American flag at the North Pole. George Borup became my most intimate friend. He was a young Yale graduate, about my own age, son of an army officer, and had distinguished himself in college athletics, particularly in the two-mile run. After returning from the North, he studied in the department of geology at the American Museum of Natural History. I met him there. His devotion to Peary and love of the Arctic were almost religious in their intensity. We used to talk hour after hour about the North Pole expedition and his plans for the future. He tried to entice me to join him and Don MacMillan in the proposed exploration of Crocker Land, but I had a project for Asia. George was drowned one brilliant Sunday afternoon in 1912 while canoeing with a friend on Long Island Sound. After surviving the dangers of the polar ice, he lost his life within sight of his summer home! My eldest son, George Borup Andrews, is named for him.

George Borup's Diary

My son had George Borup's personal diary of the North Pole expedition. He presented it to the Explorers Club in New York City. The pages are already becoming brittle and yellow, but they give an intimate picture of how Peary kept his men healthy and happy during the long winter night, and prepared for the polar dash. George's view is so fresh and uninhibited that I quote from his journal frequently.

The *Roosevelt* sailed from New York on July 6, 1908. They touched at Oyster Bay, Long Island, where the President of the United States and his family inspected the ship. George told me he was standing near the rail when Theodore Roosevelt left. He heard Peary say, "Mr. President, I shall put into this effort everything there is in me — physical, mental, and moral." The President gripped his hand and replied, "I believe in you, Peary, and I believe in your success — if it is within the possibility of man."

In a heavy sea, the ship rolled her way to the Cape Charles whaling station, on the Labrador coast, where eight tons of whale meat were taken aboard for dog food. The stench didn't help the seasick members of the party. Later, it played a sad role, for some of the dogs died from eating the half-rotten flesh.

At Cape York, Greenland, the first Eskimos were selected for the expedition. George Borup wrote: "Short, stocky and fur clad, they looked more like foxes than anything else . . . and smell! ! ! We could smell 'em a hundred yards. I looked at Mac. 'Good Lord! Have we got to live with that bunch?' But they hadn't been on board a week before we could hardly notice it at all . . .

"The men picked brought their families and dogs, and the rest were glad to trade five or six dogs for an old Springfield rifle and some shells. Peary not only speaks their lingo like a native, but also understands their feelings. When one considers that when he first came to Greenland they had practically nothing, and are now rich according to their notions; that formerly existence was precarious, where as now they have arms, boats, thread, needles and all manner of necessities, it can be readily seen that he represents something more than human to them."

Walrus Hunting

George had his first taste of walrus hunting near Cape York. He gives a graphic description of the excitement: "Holy Smoke! You may spiel of your lion shooting in Africa . . . but if you want the real thing, try a scrimmage with walrus, when everyone is standing by to repel boarders, hitting them over the heads with oars, boat-hooks, and axes, when one's decks are cleared for action and the ammunition hoist is on the bum. . . .

"A walrus when killed, will go to the bottom like some submarines, so it was up to us to get it harpooned before such events materialized. . . .

"As luck would have it, our first engagement with the

walrus was a lively session and no mistake. We'd seen about ten or more taking life easy on the ice-pan, so Captain Bob thought it was a good chance to put the tenderfeet through the ropes, and away Mac and I went with the Captain shouting instructions. . . .

"We stopped rowing a couple of hundred yards from the walrus and let Dennis Murphy, a sailor, scull us up. When within about fifty yards, every now and then a stray walrus feeding below would come up for a breath of fresh air. Sometimes they'd appear so close we could almost pat their heads with our hands.

"We didn't try to stick any of those in the water, as the ones on the pan were more promising. We wanted to row right up to them but our huskies [Eskimos] thought they were too fierce looking to get very close. While we were debating what to do, one of the heavy weights woke up, nudged another and information being passed that the police were raiding, they started for the fire escapes.

"Mac then got his Winchester automatic into play and the bullets streamed out of it like water out of a fire hose. We hit a couple and half killed another, but with a convulsive flop the brute slipped into the water. The huskies' blood was up by this time. Kyutah made a corking throw, harpooning one just as it was sinking, and another was handed out his epitaph.

"Just then about forty others came rushing up to see what all the roughhouse was about. Jerusalem! It looked as if a million whales were spouting at once. The air was full of water, cuss words and clam shells. The water was just one writhing mess of merry Hades let loose.

"Just then a trio came to the surface about fifteen yards

off. They all bore marks of the fray and were mad clean through. Giving their battle cry of 'Ook, ook!' . . . they charged us. Our magazines were as empty as a Princeton man's pockets after the Yale football game. Our huskies didn't like the look of things. They grabbed the oars, and banged them on the gunwale of the boat . . . Mac and his automatic were having a bully time and we cut loose. The walrus were treading water and banging their front flippers together. . . . The general racket, the crepitating rifles, the shouts and pounding of the huskies and the bellowing of the infuriated animals was terrific.

"We torpedoed one and knocked the propeller off another, but the biggest one dived, and the next second we were half blinded by a water spout as the giant ranged alongside and tried to give us the hook with his tusks. With the guns almost touching his head, we let 'er rip. That ended Mr. Walrus and with an exultant cheer the Eskimos threw their harpoons."

Harry Whitney, a New Haven sportsman who had paid $1500 for the privilege of going north on the *Erik*, left the ship at Cape York. It was to him that Dr. Cook said he had entrusted all his records, when he arrived in Copenhagen with nothing but his word to support his claim that he had reached the North Pole. Whitney denied that Cook had left anything with him except a few instruments to be taken back to the States.

At Etah, north of Cape York, the expedition lost the last touch with civilization. Captain Bartlett in his *The Log of Bob Bartlett* gives a vivid picture of the *Roosevelt*:

"Mixed up with the coal were 70 tons of whale meat and 246 dogs, all fighting and screaming; the dogs I mean. In addition we had 49 Eskimos and the blubber of 50 walruses. To get some idea of what this meant you must remember that the *Roosevelt* was not any bigger than the average tug. . . . To my dying day I shall never forget the frightful noise, the choking stench and the terrible confusion that reigned aboard her as we steamed slowly down Foulke Fjord and swung into the pack of Kane Basin. We had some canned peaches that night for supper; but the odor about us was so powerful that the peaches simply felt wet and cold on one's tongue, having no fruit flavor whatsoever."

The Long Arctic Night

The *Roosevelt* bucked and crashed her way through the treacherous ice in Kennedy and Robeson Channels undamaged, although often in such peril that every person had an emergency outfit on deck. At Cape Sheridan, on the coast of Grant Land, the ship went into winter quarters. From there, supplies would be sledged in relays to the ultimate land base at Cape Columbia, ninety miles away, where the dash to the Pole would start. Peary was a believer in work to keep his staff fit, mentally and physically. During the Arctic night sledging or hunting parties were out every day that the moon gave light enough to see. British explorers took quite the opposite view. One went so far as to say that a commander ought to be court-martialed for working his men during the winter. But Peary's plan paid dividends. By the coming of daylight, all the expedition were fit, and inured to the cold by outside work.

Sledging of supplies to Cape Columbia began on September 16th, and Borup writes in his diary: "The last time I

[53]

saw the sun was on Oct. 8th, though it didn't go definitely below the horizon till four days or so later." From then on, traveling was done in moonlight, but sometimes by the aid of lanterns. It was a weird business for the tenderfeet. I find this notation in Borup's journal: "Sunday, Dec. 13, 1908. My watch stopped twice and I was not sure when we left camp this morning whether it was day or night. We stopped at Henson's igloo at Cape Richardson for two hours while we 'boiled the kettle.'

"When we got to the ship I didn't know what time it was, let alone whether morning or night. The first person I saw was the Chief on deck. I asked him what time it was and what day. He said it was 4 o'clock, afternoon of Sunday Dec. 13th and that I was just in time for lunch."

Another entry: "Monday, Dec. 21st, 1908. The temperature which of late has been flirting with 40 below zero, went down to 53 below. There was no wind and we found it hard to realize it was so cold. One can always go out on deck in your undershirt for a couple of minutes without getting very cold."

The Winter Solstice

"Dec. 22, 1908. The Winter Solstice. At 4:40 A.M. the sun reached its most southern point and started back to us again . . . there was a very perceptible glow in the southern sky at noon. I suppose it could be called twilight. The Italian expedition did not see any at this time of the year, although 100 miles south of us. . . .

"The Commander wanted me to help him at the 'Feast of the Winter Solstice.' He called all the huskies, men,

[54   ]

women, and children out from their quarters on deck, drew out his watch, told them that the sun had started back, and then Marvin began to ring the ship's bell, Matt fired three shots from a revolver and I touched off ten flashlights, which performance drew loud yells from them.

"Then they came in and were given *kappa tedickshuah*, musk ox, coffee, biscuits; Marvin acted as barkeep and gave them some gin. Pengersue (16 yrs. old) was so affected . . . that he promptly got *piblockto* (crazy) and ran off in his shirt sleeves to the tide igloo to look for the sun. The men went after him, corralled the kid and brought him aboard. He got his hand well frosted; ears too. The winter has gone very fast and 'tis hard to realize it's Xmas time and the holidays are on at home."

Borup made some illuminating remarks in his diary about Peary's theory of keeping his men busy during the months of darkness: "The Arctic night, dreaded and feared by so many expeditions, the terrible depressing darkness mentioned by so many explorers, the night which drives men mad by its monotony and oppressiveness, was now half gone — almost before we knew it. Under Peary's methods, travelling during the moons, always busy on the ship, diverted by the Eskimos, if there was any monotony or dreaded darkness going the rounds, none of us crossed its trail. Constantly occupied, we were happy; the working day wasn't long enough; and I never knew until then, the real joy of living."

On his first trips in Greenland, Peary had not yet learned to build the conical snow igloos of the Eskimos, and went through much unnecessary suffering due to his inexperience. Later, he became very expert and could build an igloo as fast as a native. When winter work began, the tenderfeet of the expedition, Borup, MacMillan, and Goodsell, were sent ashore to learn the ropes of camping on ice. Borup writes: "Each Eskimo grabs his snow knife — an ugly looking affair some twelve inches long — and pokes the snow to get building material of the right consistency. . . . Then all hands fall to and begin cutting blocks. As soon as enough are on hand, one man traces an ellipse on the snow . . . As soon as two rows are up, only one man can be actually engaged in the construction while the others bring him blocks. As the walls rise, a man fills in the chinks. Putting in the last block — the key stone — is a ticklish business. A bed platform occupies the back two-thirds of the house, which is considerably higher than the floor and warmer because of the rising heat from the alcohol stove."

Peary dressed, in the main, like the Eskimos, and developed a method which enabled him to dispense entirely with the heavy sleeping bags used by all other expeditions. By drawing the *kooletah* (skin jacket) tight at the waist, and passing a string between the legs from back to front to hold it in position, and tightening the strings at the top of the *kamiks* (skin boots), the clothing could be transformed into an airtight sleeping bag. Then the arms would be slipped out of the loose sleeves and folded across the breast. Thus a man could sleep comfortably in the clothes in which he walked.

Of his first night in an igloo, George wrote: "I was amused at thinking how much my point of view had changed. We had long ago ceased to notice the huskie smell, but were still a little disinclined to getting infested with their vermin. As I lay on my musk ox robe, just before going to sleep, I looked at 'Harrigan' (Inighito in private life) who was busy swallowing the bugs off his shirt with great relish. . . . We found the best way to keep insect proof was to take off our undershirts at night, and turn them over to the huskies, offering a cigar for every scarab they caught. A successful hunt might cost four or five cigars, but it was worth the money."

Hunting at Lake Hazen

Pemmican, an "iron ration" composed of suet, meat, raisins and other ingredients, was the staple food for both men and dogs when on a sledging trip, but Peary depended upon game to give them fresh meat, which prevented the dreaded scurvy. All during the winter night, hunting parties went out from the ship to favored localities. Borup's journal has this account: "Saturday, Dec. 26, 1908. I received my marching orders for this moon. Deer [caribou] hunting, Lake Hazen, hurrah! . . . Bought two fox tails from Angodagibsu for a knife. Rather stiff price, but I wanted them bad as I am in hopes they may stop my face from getting frozen like the last time. . . .

"Dec. 29, 1908: The Captain and Marvin left after lunch for Greenland; Marvin for Cape Bryant for a month's tidal observations and the Captain for New Man Bay after musk ox. The crossing of Robeson Channel at this time of the year has never been done before."

After seven marches and a blizzard, Borup and two Eskimos reached the inland Lake Hazen on Wednesday, January 6, 1909. They found no caribou but a great number of Arctic hare, which, of course, were pure white. He writes:

[57]

"All three of us went over toward the round of the glacier, there Pan. leaving us. After quartering over the ground for a couple of hours, we saw Pan. stalking a tremendous flock, or herd, or drove, or bunch of hare. They looked to be as thick as a huge flock of little auks.

"Well, we weren't long getting into action, and finally secured 60 of them. Borup 21, Pan. 27, Ouh. 29. The hare after a shot would do a 100 or 200 yard dash, and then get up on their hind legs to see what was doing. . . . Though a brilliant full moon shone in a cloudless sky, the hare were not clearly outlined against the snow and looked like white ghosts. Their shadows were more easily seen than they were. I fired eight shots and got four — two at one shot. It was simply point at a rabbit and let 'er go, as there wasn't any use trying to sight. Pan. downed six at one crack with the shotgun, which is going some. . . .

"We laid down our guns to pick up some dead ones and saw four more between us and the guns. . . . It ended by our driving them along like a herd of sheep. They were so close that several times we tried to catch them with our hands, only to just fail. I'd have liked to try a dive tackle at one, but it was too blame rocky."

Getting their clothes made by the Eskimo women was an important feature of the preparations for the polar trip. On Saturday, January 16th, George notes: "Ootan's wife finished my seal skin *kamiks* today and Atta-ta yesterday completed my sheepskin shirt and today started on my deerskin *koolelah*. She is about the best looker on board and can sew fairly well — though they are all bum enough, Lord knows. . . . Mac came in today from the tide igloo with a poem on the subject of Atta-ta and myself. They've been guying me about her to beat the band but I'm getting my sewing done anyhow and done well. . . .

"Monday, Jan. 18th, 1909. The Commander called me into his room today and told me to get myself in A1 shape as he expected to work me like hell the first ten days of the northern trip. He said I was light and fast and he would utilize me to bring up extra dog grub while the party is within striking distance of the shore, when I will go on with the rest.

"I am beginning to feel funny in the neighborhood of my stomach — the 'elevator' feeling of my track days at Yale — with all the preparations being pushed for the spring trip. I feel as though I were back in the track house at Yale waiting for the cry, 'First call for the two mile,' then the tinkle of the 'phone ten minutes later, and 'last call for the two mile.' Then to hell with the nervous feeling when the pistol cracks and you get into action."

Plan for the Polar Dash

As a result of his long experience, Peary had worked out a paper plan for his attack on the Pole. It consisted of five cooperating but independent parties, four of which acted in support of the fifth, which was the commander's. The others were designed to put him at the ultimate advanced base on the sea ice, less than one hundred and fifty miles from the Pole. Then, with the pick of sleds, dogs, and drivers, he would make the final dash and return to land in forced marches over the outward trail, utilizing the igloos and supplies cached at the various stations.

Had the terrain been immovable land as in the Antarctic,

it would have been "foolproof." But over the shifting sea ice of the Arctic basin an element of chance, for which no amount of planning could provide, entered into any campaign. The possibility, even probability, that storms would open leads, the ice shift, and the trail be lost, was ever present. That happened on his previous (1906) expedition, when a strong drift of the ice to the east completely disrupted his plan. He could only depend upon God and pray for good weather.

The ever present "Big Lead" or "Grand Canal" loomed as the greatest hazard. By starting as soon as the light was strong enough to travel, in temperatures from thirty to sixty degrees below zero, the leads would freeze quickly unless kept open by high winds. But on the return journey, made nearly two months later in warmer weather, freezing would be slower and floe movements greater, particularly with the full moon at the end of April. Therefore, supply depots must be laid down in each direction on the Grant Land and Greenland coasts, so if the polar party were driven off their course and reached land, they would find food. Lacking this in 1906, Peary had nearly starved to death.

On February 15, with a lantern, Captain Bartlett left the ship for the polar jumping-off place at Cape Columbia. All the other members of the expedition followed within a few days. It was cold at Columbia — 57 below zero. As George and Mac came in, Peary greeted them by saying: "Borup, your face is frozen. MacMillan, your nose is gone."

George wrote: "Sat., Feb. 27th, 1909. 50 below zero. Last night was one of the coldest I ever spent. It was so bad the huskies couldn't sleep even though both stoves were going full blast. . . . I found I was to start out in the morning as a pioneer advance supporting party with the Captain and his men with one sledge to break the way. This is *It*.

"After grub, the Commander gave us a short talk. He mentioned that the next six weeks would be undiluted hell, the only variation in the monotony being that occasionally it would get worse. He told us to cheer up, however, when we thought of those sandy Italians facing 52 below zero (Centigrade) in woolen clothing, tents, and 48 pound sleeping bags."

The next day they started the polar dash. "Sunday, Feb. 28. This was one of the hardest days work I have ever put in and at the end of it I was more all in than ever I was at the end of a two mile race. Though fifty below, and wearing my light sheepskin shirt, I was soon in a reeking sweat. . . . The going was the worst I struck while out to sea. . . ."

At the end of the second day Bartlett, as Peary had directed, sent Borup back to Cape Columbia to bring up more supplies, while he went on to break trail. The relay system worked well, but early in the dash, one unforeseen event nearly caused complete disaster. Some of the alcohol tins broke open at the seams, and not enough remained to take Peary to the Pole and back. Without heat, the whole expedition might well be ruined. Marvin and Borup were instructed by notes left in the igloos, to bring oil and alcohol at top speed to the commander, who was forty miles out on the sea ice and going forward every day. Five miles from Cape Columbia they were stopped by open water. Borup writes: "Friday, March 5, 1909. There stretched a lead, four hundred yards wide in either direction as far as the eye could see. The huskies went out east and west scouting, but no use — the lead seemed equally wide everywhere.

Crossing was impossible. It was case of sit down and wait for the lead either to close or freeze.

Stopped at the Big Lead

"The delay was heartbreaking for we knew how vitally important it was to get out to the Commander with the fuel, grub and the splendid dogs in our party. Yet we couldn't do a thing. It wasn't the physical side—it was the mental side of the game which was undiluted hell just then. . . .

"The ice on the far side of the lead was drifting steadily eastward, although there was no wind.

"March 6th. The lead has widened. If stationary, it would have frozen over strong enough in twenty-four hours for us to cross, but it drifted apart just fast enough to keep a strip of open water in the middle, which smoked like coke ovens in the stinging air. The only comfort was the first sight of the *Sun*. At mid-day we were sitting in our igloo having a cup of tea. A small peep hole had been cut in the side of the house looking south. Suddenly, through the hole, a beam of light came falling right on my head. The men jumped to their feet yelling '*Suck-in-nuck!*, *Suck-in-nuck!*.' We streaked outside our igloo. Marvin and his men were yelling too! Five months since we had seen it! It certainly looks *Great!*"

For five days Borup and Marvin sat there nearly frantic with anxiety. By that time, Peary would be more than ninety miles out at sea, and even if they did get across they were not sure they could recover his trail. George writes: ". . . besides knowing that the success or failure of the ex-

pedition might depend on our catching the other, we also
knew that if we did not get out we could never explain it,
and at home there would always be the question of someone having lost his nerve."

On March 10th, the lead closed and the men rushed
ahead. Borup froze one heel, but kept going at full speed.
He wrote: "I've had my troubles all right — a large blister
forming on the heel and every step I took felt as if a trip
hammer had hit it. But it wasn't any worse than trying to
run when you are all in."

Rejoining Peary

On the fourteenth they caught up with Peary, who had
been delayed by open water. Borup wrote in his journal:
"In the bitter air and intense silence, we could hear the
yelping of the dogs of the main party hours before we
sighted the longed-for camp, perched high on a knoll of
ice. Lord, how good it looked! A few hundred yards from
camp I saw the Commander coming out to meet me. When
we shook hands it was the proudest and happiest moment
of my life."

MacMillan had frozen his heel the morning of the
eleventh, and it had festered and was in very bad shape.
He had to return the following day. It was heartbreaking
for him. George says:

"Just before turning in, Marvin and I joined the Captain
and Mac in their igloo for about fifteen minutes and we
had a final song '*Amici usque*' but we couldn't sing it as we
had two weeks before at Cape Columbia. Mac was too
downhearted, and so were we, at his bad luck. Then we

broke up. As Marvin and I went to our respective igloos, we shook hands. 'Cornell always was strong on cross country,' I remarked, and he said, 'Yes, that's so. But it hasn't been a two mile race nor even a cross-country one. It's been a Marathon and a damn long one.' "

The polar dash proceeded according to schedule. Every five marches someone went back. Dr. Goodsell was first, then MacMillan, Borup, Marvin, and Bartlett. Henson and Peary went to the Pole.

On March 20, Borup turned southward at latitude 85° 23′ N. He wrote: "This was my fartherest north. I would have given my immortal soul to have gone on. I was in luck to get as far as I did. As a matter of fact, the Commander lugged some of us a good deal farther than necessary, knowing our feelings. I never felt so bad in my life as when I turned my footsteps landward, and I hope I never will again. Still, it was part of the game. . . .

"I'll never forget my last goodby to Marvin. He was lying on the bed-platform of his igloo resting up, waiting to take a shot at the sun at noon. As I crawled in through the door he gave me a slip of instructions as to what grub I was to cache at Cape Fanshaw. Our talk was short. Somehow one doesn't feel like it on such occasions. I said I hoped Peary would take him to the Pole, but he wasn't hoping for any such luck, as there wasn't enough food. Then we shook hands, and I said we'd meet inside a month."

Bartlett Turns Back

Peary made good progress with Bartlett and Henson. According to schedule, five marches after Marvin left, the captain turned back. On the last morning he took an observation. The position was 87° 46′ 49″ N. Then he walked ahead a few miles, hoping to cross the 88° parallel, but did not quite succeed. He had come farther north than any other human being up to that time; still, he turned southward with a heavy heart.

Peary has been severely criticized for not taking Bartlett to the Pole, but he had good reasons. It might well be that none of the men on the final dash would survive. No one except Peary or Bartlett had sufficient experience to pilot the *Roosevelt* out through the pack ice. If both were lost, the lives of the rest of the party would be in jeopardy. Moreover, Henson was the best dog driver of anyone in the expedition except the Eskimos. Peary said of him, "He is the most nearly indispensable man with whom I have ever been associated." In his foreword to the book *Dark Companion*, Don MacMillan said Henson was selected "because he was a better man than any of us." Moreover, Bartlett, as a Canadian, was a British subject, and had he gone to the Pole the honor of discovery would have been shared by two nations. Even though Bartlett admitted that he would have given anything to go on, he always stoutly defended Peary's decision not to take him.

When the captain left, Peary was in a favorable position for the final dash. He had five sleds, all in good condition, forty dogs, the pick of the entire lot, and ample food. His four native drivers were the best of all the Eskimos, and had proved their stamina, loyalty, and ability. If weather continued favorable, and the party were not held up by open water, it would be possible to reach the Pole in five marches.

Peary and Henson pushed forward at top speed over good ice, sleeping only three or four hours between marches. On the night of April 5th, the party was pretty well played out and more sleep was taken. A latitude observation at this camp showed they were thirty-five miles from the Pole. A start was made before midnight, in an air temperature of only fifteen degrees below zero. After a run of thirty miles on smooth ice, camp was made and named Camp Morris K. Jesup, in honor of Peary's great friend and backer. Noon observations showed it to be three miles from the Pole. With two Eskimos, Egingwah and Seegloo, driving a double team of dogs, Peary took his instruments and went on for an estimated ten miles. A midnight observation of the sun showed he had gone beyond the Pole. Of this he wrote in his diary: "When I had taken my observations at Camp Jesup in the Western Hemisphere at noon of April 6th, Columbia meridian time, the sun had been in the south. When I had taken my observations at midnight between the 6th and 7th, at the end of my ten mile march in the Eastern Hemisphere, the sun was in the south at that point — but to those at the camp on the other side of the world only ten miles away, it was in the north."

The Pole at Last, April 6, 1909

Peary returned to Camp Morris K. Jesup and on the morning of the seventh took another series of observations, at right angles to those already made there, and sledged another eight miles. Other observations followed. He wrote: "I had now taken thirteen single or six and one-half double altitudes of the sun at two different stations in three different directions, at four different times." To allow for possible errors in instruments and observations, he traversed in various directions an area of about eight by ten miles. At some moment during these marches and counter-marches, he had for all practical purposes passed over the point where north and south and east and west blend into one.

"Though recognizing that no one was ever likely to find them, two records and a diagonal strip from his silken flag were placed in a snow cairn. One document took possession of the region in the name of the President of the United States. The American and other flags were raised and cheered at this, the first and only Pole of the earth ever reached by man," Dr. Hobbs writes.

Peary has written: "If it were possible for a man to arrive at 90 degrees north latitude without being utterly exhausted, body and brain, he would doubtless enjoy a series of unique sensations and reflections. But the attainment of the Pole was the culmination of days and weeks of forced marches, physical discomfort, insufficient sleep, and racking anxiety. It is a wise provision of nature that the human consciousness can grasp only such degree of intense feeling as the brain can endure, and the grim guardians of earth's remotest spot will accept no man as guest until he has been tried and tested by the severest ordeal."

Now the question was, could the party return to land before the next spring tides, only three weeks away, opened the leads and cut them off? The dogs were extra-rationed, and everything was discarded that was not absolutely essential. Peary's plan was to make double marches on the return journey, thus covering the distance in half the outward time. Fortune favored them. They followed the trail with little difficulty, utilizing the igloos, crossed the "Big Lead" on new ice, and before midnight of April 22nd, the party climbed up on the firm glacial fringe of Grant Land. When the last sledge rested safely, the Eskimos went almost crazy with delight. Peary said: "They yelled and called and danced until they fell in utter exhaustion. As Oo-tah sank down on his sledge he remarked in Eskimo: 'The devil is asleep or having trouble with his wife, or we should never have come back so easily.' "

Death of Ross Marvin

Arriving at the Cape Columbia base, known as "Crane City," the dogs were each given four pounds of pemmican and the men ate and slept, ate and slept for forty-eight hours continuously. Then they went on to the ship. When Peary reached the *Roosevelt*, he was met by Bartlett bringing the sad news of Marvin's death. Peary was staggered. This, the first blow to take the joy out of his successful effort, fell with tragic suddenness. He wrote: "It was hard to realize at first that the man who had worked at my side through so many weary months under conditions of peril and privation, to whose efforts and example so much of the success of the expedition had been due, would never stand beside me again. . . ."

Ross Marvin was the only casualty Peary had had among his active staff during twenty-three years in the Arctic.

Mystery still envelops Marvin's death. The story, as Borup's diary records it, is as follows. Borup was on the *Roosevelt* at Cape Sheridan. "It was midnight of April 17th, that the familiar cry of *kamuttee* coming (a sledge coming) rang out and we knew that Marvin's division was at hand. Now, ordinarily, the dogs come tearing in as fast as they can lick it, but these came at a funeral pace, and Marvin's red toque nowhere to be seen. I thought it strange that he would let the Eskimos pass him so near the ship, and yet couldn't believe anything had happened till Jack Barnes, who was taking tidal observations, ran out from the igloo, spoke to one of the men, and then turned as white as the snow on which he stood. Then I reached Kudlooktoo.

" 'Marvin's gone. Young ice. I tol' him look out. I tol' him look out,' said he, in a broken voice, pointing downward . . . We couldn't realize it. It was too horrible to be true. Poor Marvin!

"We got Kudlooktoo, who was a trifle more collected than 'Harrigan,' the other man who had come back in Marvin's division, into the mess room and began to talk to him. Marvin had gone on five more marches and had turned back the 25th of March. Open water had prevented him from double marching for several days — in fact they only made three miles in as many days on that account. Besides the trail was badly faulted.

"They recovered it near the fifth encampment on the outward journey, and the next morning Marvin, as usual, set out ahead of his men, as the rest of us had done. A few miles beyond lay the Big Lead, and when Kudlooktoo and Harrigan arrived they saw the back of his *kooletah* floating above the water. The air in it held poor Marvin up. They

[69]

tried to get him out, but the ice was too thin and to their repeated calls he gave no answer. He had evidently made a fine fight for his life, as the ice was broken in a circle ten yards in diameter, where he had made game and repeated efforts to get out.

"They camped on the nearest old ice and the next morning found that his body had gone down. Near this hole, in accordance with their custom of not having things around belonging to one who has gone, they disposed of his bag which contained all the specimens of the bottom that the soundings had brought up, but luckily they had not thrown away his note book. One sleep, and they reached Columbia, had two sleeps there, and three more brought them aboard."

In the summer of 1926, my friend the late George Palmer Putnam, while on an expedition to the Arctic, learned that Kudlooktoo had become a Christian. When he was baptized and made confession, he stated that he had shot and killed Marvin. Harrigan, his companion at the time, confirmed the story. Kudlooktoo said that Marvin was displeased at something Harrigan had done, and threatened to leave him behind without food. That meant starvation. In order to save his friend, he had killed the white man. Putnam wired the story to the *New York Times*, and it was given great prominence. Other members of the expedition then living all agreed that it was preposterous to think Marvin would have done such a thing. He was a fine man, of even temper, and knew the Eskimos better than anyone else except Peary. To my mind, it is more credible that Kudlooktoo had become temporarily *piblockto*, stricken with the dread Arctic craziness that attacks both men and dogs when they have been subject to great strain, and that he invented the excuse for his act of murder.

Of *piblockto* Peary says: "The immediate cause of this affection is hard to trace, though sometimes it seems to be the result of brooding over absent or dead relatives, or a fear of the future. The manifestations of this disease are somewhat startling. The patient, usually a woman, begins to scream and tear or destroy her clothing. If on the ship, she will walk up and down the deck, screaming and gesticulating, and generally is in a state of nudity, though the thermometer may be in the minus forties. As the intensity of the attack increases she will sometimes leap over the rail upon the ice, running perhaps half a mile. The attack may last a few minutes, an hour, or even more, and some sufferers become so wild that they will continue running about on the ice perfectly naked until they freeze to death, if they are not forcibly brought back. . . . The attack usually ends in a fit of weeping, and when the patient quiets down, the eyes are bloodshot, the pulse high and the whole body trembles for an hour or so afterwards."

A note in George Borup's diary, made when he and Mac-Millan were on the trip to Greenland to lay down caches while Peary was at the Pole, indicates that Kudlooktoo was an unstable individual. "Friday, April 30, 1909. Mac and I were quite worried about Kudlooktoo for awhile. Yesterday, he dumped half his load off a little beyond where we had placed the half loads the day before. After supper he went back for the rest of his load but twelve hours later he had not appeared. We thought it possible that he was heading for the boat or had met a bear. But suddenly he returned. He had put in the night sleeping on his sledge."

First News of Cook's Claim

The *Roosevelt* was released from her berth at Cape Sheridan when the ice broke up on July 18th, and made her way through the pack in Robeson Channel with little difficulty.

Borup writes: "At Nerke, the first place we touched, we heard that Dr. Cook had come back early in the spring with his two boys and that he had told the white men at Etah he had been a long way out on the sea ice and that he'd gotten far north, but the natives said he'd lied; that Itukishoo and Apilah had said they had gone no distance north over the sea-ice. As for Dr. Cook, he'd gone to South Greenland."

George wrote in his diary that they did not take the reports of Cook's trip seriously until they reached Etah. There Itukishoo and Apilah, Cook's Eskimo companions, came aboard. He says, "We pretended to know they had been far north and tried to make them admit they'd been ten or fifteen marches out to sea and no land visible, but they stood by their statements that they'd been only two marches out in the direction of Dr. Cook's Boreal Center.

"Ashore, we saw the sledge Cook had used. The Eskimos said this sledge, and they, had been inseparable companions during the whole trip from Etah to their fartherest two marches north of Cape Hubbard, back to Cape Sparbo and to Etah. Except for its being shortened, the sledge was the same as when it had left Anoratok. Now it weighed probably thirty pounds and was very flimsy — yet had only two cracks in it.

"The casualties among our *kamuttees* (sledges) on the first day's march from Columbia, were two so wrecked that their owners had to go back after new ones, and about six fairly well laid out, and not a day's march but what a lot were badly damaged, till finally, on the 16th of March, Henson's party broke all three of theirs so badly they had to build two new ones out of the three derelicts!

"Our sledges weighed seventy-five pounds on an average, and the larger ones ninety-five and with their solid runners were infinitely stronger than the one shown us as having been used by Cook. So one glance was enough to show us it couldn't have tasted much polar ice. Old Ootah, of the North Pole party, glanced at Cook's sledge with a scornful grin."

This is interesting in the light of Cook's claim that he sledged from Cape Thomas Hubbard to the Pole and back — 1040 geographical miles across sea ice, or 214 miles more than Peary's entire sledge journey — without either supporting parties or anything in the way of supplies beyond what was carried upon two sleds.

Still only partially believing the rumors, Peary and the whole staff were stunned to learn, at Indian Harbor, Labrador, the details of Cook's reception in Copenhagen. Seething with indignation, he dispatched his ill-fated telegrams to the United Press and the *New York Times* on September 6th, but they did not get through until the eighth.

Cook's Records Rejected

While Cook was in the midst of the orgy of hasty approval in Denmark, the Royal Danish Geographical Society and the University of Copenhagen asked him to submit his observations of the sun taken at the Pole, together with the diary of his dog-sledge journey. Cook replied that these precious documents, the only records that could substantiate his claim, he had given to Harry Whitney in Greenland, and they would be submitted later. It seems incredible that those distinguished societies would have accepted such an astounding statement even temporarily. When Whitney stated that Cook had given him nothing but some instruments, Cook replied, "It doesn't make any difference because I have copies." *Only the originals, of course, would have any value.*

Months later, he did submit a so-called "copy" of his notebook and other data, and these were rejected by the university. Dr. Stromgen, the eminent astronomer and chairman of the examining body of experts, said: "Cook's action is shameless. It was an offense to submit such papers to scientific men." Dr. Rasmussen remarked: "The University would not call me at first, because I was one of Dr. Cook's strongest supporters. Later, however, I was invited to the investigation, and when I saw the observations I realized it was a scandal. But the papers which Cook sent to Copenhagen are most impudent."

Rasmussen, who, by the way, is part Eskimo and has lived among Eskimos most of his life, later interviewed Cook's two natives, whom he knew well. They gave him exactly the same story they had told Peary, and stoutly maintained that Cook had gone no more than two marches northward out on the sea ice. This statement Rasmussen made public.

Pressure on Cook to produce some tangible proof that he had reached the Pole became so great that he began to hedge. Dr. Hobbs says that in January, 1910, before a group of newspapermen, he spoke of his possible "delusion" concerning the Pole. Shortly afterward he disappeared into the Southern Hemisphere and took an assumed name. Almost a year later he returned, bringing a manuscript, "My Attainment of the Pole," which he sold for a large figure, first to *Hampton's Magazine* and then as a book.

Hobbs continues: "In a press interview shortly after his return, Cook asserted that he 'might' have reached the Pole. Later, in a lecture at Harlem, he declared he was 'more positive than ever' that he had reached the Pole. 'Within my own bosom,' he is reported to have said, 'there is the satisfying thump of success won at great cost.' In his lectures, his denunciation of Peary was in such violent language as to draw loud applause from the galleries."

While Cook was in the Arctic, the investigation of his claim to have reached the summit of Mt. McKinley was undertaken by a committee of the Explorers Club, for it was seriously doubted. It was suspended until after he had returned and his book had been published. The investigation was then resumed. Cook came before the committee with a lawyer and agreed to answer the charges within ten days, but he did not appear. The committee heard testimony from the guide who accompanied Cook and from other members of the expedition. Then Professor Hershell Parker of Columbia University and Belmore Brown, two distinguished mountain climbers, followed the trail outlined in his book step by step. They discovered that his "summit" was many miles from the peak of Mt. McKinley. Cook was expelled from the Explorers Club, of which he had been a president, from the Arctic Club and from the Council of the Brooklyn Institute of Arts and Sciences.

Cook's Posthumous Book

Cook's last attempt at continuing his polar myth is his posthumous book *Return from the Pole*, published at the end of 1951.

Vilhjalmur Stefanssen, the foremost living authority on the Arctic and the greatest ice traveler of modern times, not excepting Peary, has reviewed the book in *Natural History*. He says in part: "That Robert E. Peary had reached the Pole on April 6, 1909, as told in his 1910 book, *The North Pole*, was in due course generally accepted. That Cook had made up a Robinson Crusoe yarn, told in 1911 in *My Attainment of the Pole* was the conclusion of nearly everybody, including all the reference works. When Cook's friends, in his name, brought one libel suit after another against the publishers and authors of encyclopedias, histories, and biographies, the suits were thrown out of court. The insufficiency of Cook's narrative, and of his explanations is thus among the few issues in polar explorations that have been passed on by courts as well as critics. From the heights, Cook went to the depths, and finally to Leavenworth prison for using the mails to defraud — however on an issue that had nothing to do with exploration.

"Cook has always made friends. Peary liked him when he had him as surgeon in the Greenland Arctic in 1891–92; he was the most popular member of the Belgian Antarctic Expedition of 1898–99; in Leavenworth he was nearly or quite the best liked prisoner, with both inmates and staff. After serving only a part of his term he was paroled in 1930 and immediately began that pathetic try for a comeback which is represented by the present book. For we are told by the editor: 'Dr. Cook wrote *Return from the Pole* in long-hand, beginning it in 1930 and completing it in 1935 when he was seventy years of age!' "

Cook did a great disservice to exploration as a whole. After the controversy, the public looked askance at every explorer, no matter what his background, and viewed even the smallest discoveries with suspicion. Moreover, that America did not have the honor of first flying the Stars and Stripes at the southernmost point of the earth as well as at the northernmost, was probably due to Frederick A. Cook. While Peary was still in the Arctic, he had outlined a plan for an immediate attack on the South Pole, using the Weddel Sea coast as a base, instead of the traditional Ross Sea. The *Roosevelt*, the finest ice ship in the world, was ready. Bartlett as leader, assisted by Borup and MacMillan, formed the nucleus of a trained staff. Using the methods developed by Peary in the north, and which Amundsen successfully employed, they could have romped to the South Pole as he did. Peary, and the National Geographic Society, tried to inaugurate the expedition, but the raging Cook-Peary dispute effectively blocked every attempt to arouse public interest. About $10,000 was subscribed, but the society eventually returned it to the donors.

Awards to Peary

When Peary's records and observations were examined and accepted by the most distinguished geographers in America, appointed by the National Geographic Society, he left his Eagle Island home in Maine, and moved to Washington. A special gold medal was awarded to him "for his dis-

covery of the North Pole." Cables of congratulation arrived from scientific institutions and eminent persons all
over the world. Other American geographic societies honored him. On February 8, 1910, the City of New York gave
him a great public testimonial in the Metropolitan Opera
House and the following April, in response to many invitations to lecture, he sailed for Europe. It was a triumphal
tour and must have done much to assuage the hurt given
him in his own country. He spoke in London, Rome, Vi-
enna, Budapest, Berlin, St. Petersburg, Paris, Brussels, Ant-
werp, Dublin and Edinburgh. Everywhere he was received
with the greatest enthusiasm and awarded special medals.
In Berlin, Professor Albrect Penck, in making the geographical society's award, said: "We celebrate not alone the hero
who has reached the Pole but an investigator who has
cleared up a great deal of the polar region." Following custom, the Royal Geographic Society of London made its
own investigations of Peary's records and reached the same
conclusion as had the American experts.

The Government of the United States honored Peary,
but not without vitriolic debate that saddened him greatly.
In February, 1910, a month after the Copenhagen authorities had rejected Cook's claim, Senator Hale of Maine
introduced a bill in the Senate recommending that the
President of the United States appoint Peary a rear admiral
in the Civil Engineers' Corps of the navy, and place him on
the retired list with the highest pay of the grade. The Senate passed this bill unanimously. In the House of Representatives a similar bill, sponsored by Bates, was referred to a
subcommittee of the large Naval Affairs Committee. Professor Hobbs writes: "This action marked the beginning of

one of the most discreditable proceedings in the history of that body. At once the old disputation was revived, only more intensified because more definitely concentrated. The Committee was bombarded by letters from Cook partisans denouncing Peary and demanding that nothing in the nature of a reward be given him. Within the Navy Department itself, opposition flared up from a group of officers, mainly of the line, who objected to having anyone "jumped" over them for promotion. . . .

"Prominent in the opposition, was Rear-Admiral Schley, one of the most active partisans of Cook who had sponsored his triumphal entry into New York and, after stating publicly that he would abide by the decision at Copenhagen, refused to do so. Far more potent, however, in its effect on public opinion was the hostile attitude of General Greely, who had commanded the ill-fated Lady Franklin Bay Expedition, one of the largest and certainly the most disastrous ever sent by the United States to the arctic."

The Bates Bill was reported out from the Naval Affairs Committee of the House unfavorably, and nothing more was done at that session of Congress. When Peary returned from his triumphal tour of Europe, he was automatically advanced from the rank of commander to that of captain upon examination. Then some of the naval officers who were opposed to him stated that he had not complied with the requirement that officers must be able to travel on horseback ninety miles in three successive days. (Why, in Heaven's name, a naval officer should be required to *ride a horse* to show physical fitness is more than I have ever been able to explain.) That was "duck soup" for Peary. Although he had not been in a saddle in seventeen years, he had been an expert horseman in his youth. He could thumb his nose at his naval critics when, in the test, he rode one hundred seventeen miles in the allotted time — twenty-seven miles farther than the required distance.

President Taft Recommends Recognition by Congress

When the 63rd Congress opened on December 6, 1910, President Taft, in his Second Annual Message, included these words: "The complete success of our country in Arctic exploration should not remain unnoticed. . . . The unparalleled accomplishment of an American in reaching the North Pole, April 6, 1909, approved by the most expert scientists, has added to the distinction of our Navy, to which he belongs, and reflects credit upon his country. His unique success has received generous acknowledgement from scientific bodies and institutions of learning in Europe and America. I recommend fitting recognition by Congress of the great achievement of Robert E. Peary."

Even after this Representative Macon stated he would fight any honor to Peary to the last ditch, since "there was no more proof that Peary discovered the Pole than Dr. Cook had to his assertion."

During examination before the naval affairs subcommittee, Peary was heckled and humiliated in every possible way by the politicians favoring Cook. After the bill was reported out favorably, Representative Macon spoke against it for an hour and one half of vituperation on the floor of the House, and Representative Helgesen of North Dakota declared Peary to be "the greatest faker which ever disgraced the nation."

Eventually Peary was commissioned a rear admiral in the Civil Engineers Corps of the navy, placed upon the retired list, and given the thanks of Congress for his discovery of the North Pole. After the ordeal which he had endured, he might well have thought that "a prophet is without honor in his own country." In all, Peary received twenty-six medals and trophies for his Arctic explorations, and four honorary degrees. In 1920, a United States torpedo-boat destroyer was christened *Peary*.

Peary Advocates Air Power

From 1910 until his death, Peary became an active advocate of airplane development. Speaking at a dinner of the Aero Club in 1912, he said: "I have no hesitation in saying that aeroplanes will not only cross the Atlantic and fly around the world, but cruise to the North Pole across the polar basin within a very short time."

Peary saw the vitally important place of air power in national defense and, before the beginning of World War I, was indefatigable in attempts to bring this need before the public. At that time there were less than twenty aviators in the army and navy combined, and not that number of planes. Peary strongly advocated an aerial coast patrol, and made speaking trips all over the country in behalf of the project. It was more through his efforts than any other man's that President Wilson approved the plan.

During the years from 1910 to 1916, I saw Peary frequently. He had been president of the Explorers Club since 1907, and I was on a committee with him to acquire the *Roosevelt* for expedition use and, eventually, as a permanent historical exhibit. The Norwegians did that with Nansen's *Fram*. Peary loved the ship which he had designed and built, and the project was very near his heart. We spent hours discussing ways and means. We tried to get the United States Government to buy it, but Cook's adherents in Congress ruined that plan. Attempts at popular subscription got nowhere, for Cook was actively campaigning against anything concerned with Peary. Cook had gone into vaudeville and devoted most of his "act" to vilifying Peary. World War I finally put an end to our attempts. Eventually the *Roosevelt* was sold to a commercial concern.

When Peary came to New York, I used to meet him at the Explorers Club or the American Museum. The picture Cook had painted of Peary, and which he endeavored to instill in the public mind, was of a ruthless martinet, utterly cold and imperious. Nothing could be further from the man's real character. I found him naturally reserved and rather grave, but kindly and sympathetic and always ready to advise me in my personal problems of exploration, some of which I brought to him. He was frank, perhaps too frank, and did not mince words when discussing a situation or a person, but was never vindictive even about Cook, who had done him mortal wrong. The men of his expedition respected him and loved him devotedly. Those who worked with him in the field can best tell what sort of a man he was. Bartlett wrote: "In every emergency . . . he always thought of the welfare of his men first and of himself last. . . . I know of innumerable cases where he denied himself necessities to supply his men. . . . He was the same unchangeable Peary through stress and difficulties which try men's souls, and through difficulties which seemed almost insurmountable. He was kindness and thoughtfulness personified."

George Borup said: "What a leader to serve under! Always kind, considerate, giving us fellows good advice, going out of his way to help us."

MacMillan tells how, when he had fallen through the ice at 59 below zero, Peary "beat the ice from my bearskin pants, pulled off my boots, and wiped my feet and legs with the inside of his warm shirt."

Death of a Hero

In 1917, after Peary returned from a grueling speaking tour, in which he tried to bring home to the American people the magnitude of the struggle that lay before them in the war, his doctors told him he had pernicious anemia. No cure had been discovered for the disease. Peary knew the verdict was a sentence of death, but he continued his work beyond the limit of his strength. He died on February 20, 1920, in Washington, and was buried in Arlington Cemetery with naval honors and impressive ceremonies. Dr. Hobbs tells how two years later, on April 6, 1922, the thirteenth anniversary of the discovery of the Pole, a memorial was dedicated to him in the presence of the President of the United States, Cabinet members, officials of the navy and army and diplomatic corps, representatives of hundreds of scientific societies, and prominent citizens from all over the country. Such a distinguished gathering had not come together since the Armistice Day ceremonies for the Unknown Soldier.

"The monument over his grave, provided by the National Geographic Society, is a massive oblate spheroid of white granite from Maine, representing the Earth with the continental outlines indicated, and at the North Pole a bronze star. On one side of the base is cut Peary's life motto, *Inveniam viam aut faciam* (I shall find a way or make one)."

There were other memorials, but the one which, I think, Peary would have liked best, is that erected by his friends: a towering stone column, fifty-three feet high, which stands on a promontory at Cape York, Greenland, the American gateway to the Pole. On the three sides of the triangular shaft the letter "P" is deeply incised.

Professor Hobbs has written for him a fitting epitaph. "As Harold Sverdrup said of Fridtjof Nansen: 'He was a great man as an explorer . . . He was greater as a man.' He went through a fiery furnace of vituperative attack and inquisition set on foot by the Cook controversy, and he emerged from the suffering unembittered, the same unchanging Peary, one of the great of all nations and of all time."

Aftermath

Excerpt from *The Explorers Journal*, Summer 1952, Vol. XXX, No. 3, published by the Explorers Club of New York City:

PEARY'S SIGNBOARDS STILL POINT WAY TO NORTH POLE
Rear Admiral Robert E. Peary, U.S.N. (Ret.), dis-

coverer of the North Pole, left long-standing guide-posts for the men who today follow his track across the top of the world. His records and supply boxes, found recently by U.S. Air Force fliers on Cape Columbia, are not the first of such caches to come to light, according to the National Geographic Society. But the newest discovery may prove to be the most historic.

It was on Cape Columbia, northernmost land tip of Canada that the explorer in June, 1909, built a final marker before turning homeward from his hard-won conquest of the North Pole. A stone cairn was erected, holding a sign-post of sledge planks pointing due North, East, South and West. This was supported by heavy guy wires and carried directions and distances punched into copper plates. Below the arms of the sign, in a frame covered with glass to protect it from the weather, a notice was placed, dated June 12, 1909:

This monument marks the point of departure and return of the sledge expedition of the Peary Arctic Club, which in the Spring of 1909 attained the North Pole.

The members of the expedition taking part in the sledge work were Peary, Bartlett, Goodsell, Marvin, MacMillan, Borup, Henson.

The various sledge divisions left here February 28th and March 1st, and returned from March 18th to April 23rd.

The Club's Steamer *Roosevelt* wintered at C. Sheridan, 73 miles east of here. [Peary later gave this distance as 93 miles.]

The placard was followed by a list of the expedition members and ship's crew, plus a tragic footnote of Marvin: "Drowned April 10th, returning from 86° 38′ N. Lat."

First in 1906 and again in 1909, Peary set out from Ellesmere Island across the frozen ocean toward the long-sought 90° North. Smashed sledges, hastily built snow houses and discarded supplies marked his difficult trail.

In moving his supplies from the *Roosevelt* up to his jumping-off points, Peary also twice established a chain of relay stations along the northern land rim. Thus the entire 500-mile route was dotted by material evidence of his expeditions.

In 1906, reaching a "Fartherest North" of 87° 6′, he built a cache. In 1909, at the Pole itself, he left documents and a strip of his flag in a glass bottle wedged between two ice blocks. It is not likely that these markers still survive on the drifting ever changing ice.

MACMILLAN FINDS MARKER

After returning to land in 1906, however, Peary pushed westward, away from the ship, and left a cairn on Cape Thomas Hubbard at the northern tip of Axel Heiberg Island. Both this and Peary's Cape Sheridan markers have been found, the first by Donald Mac-Millan in 1914, the last by a Navy-Coast Guard task force in 1948.

Still awaiting discovery is a Peary cache at Cape Morris Jesup on Greenland's Arctic coast, at the world's northernmost point of land. On a mountain peak at Cape Columbia, in addition, is a cairn holding a tin can with a piece of Peary's flag and a record of his 1906 expedition inside.

PEARY'S WIDOW IS 89

The widow of Rear Admiral Robert E. Peary, discoverer of the North Pole, was 89 years old on May
22, 1952. Mrs. Peary was the first white woman to
accompany an Arctic expedition. She was with her
husband on several trips north before he discovered
the Pole.

Akeley of Africa

I RETURNED to the American Museum of Natural History in New York near the end of 1925, after a year in the Far East. The first man I met in the foyer was Carl Akeley. I literally hugged him, for there were few men who inspired such deep affection among his friends as "Ake."

"What's doing, Ake?" I asked him. "Are you coming or going or staying?"

"Leaving soon, Roy," he said. "In a month we sail for British East. African Hall is a real going concern. It's been a long fight, but at last it's over the top. Come up to my room."

I went. In the half light of a partitioned hall that served Akeley as a studio, an elephant bulked hugely almost to the ceiling. Two life-sized statues of Nandi warriors in bronze poised with spears and shields against a pair of charging lions. A white rhinoceros stood in majestic repose beside the window. The floor was strewn with a mass of half-packed equipment, boxes and debris. An elephant gun lay on the desk.

We picked our way through the litter and sat down. Puffing on a brown pipe, Ake told me of his efforts in the last year to obtain financial support for his greatest work, the African Hall.

"I have five men who have made themselves financially responsible for six groups," he said. "George Eastman and Dan Pomeroy are going to Africa with me for the beginning. We'll get lion, buffalo, giraffe and kudu. Mr. Eastman particularly wants to shoot the buffalo."

He motioned toward the model of the hall which he had constructed soon after the plan took form in his mind. Everything was in miniature to scale — the groups, murals, floor bronzes — just as the hall would appear in its completed form. "Now, that will be a reality. I can hardly believe it."

But in spite of his infectious enthusiasm, at 61 Akeley looked like a really old man. His massive shoulders sagged and his face was lined with deep furrows etched by fatigue and suffering. A white scar ran in a jagged line across his cheek. A raging bull elephant was responsible for that. As he threw up his right arm in a gesture, the shirt sleeve fell away and I saw the marks left by the teeth of a leopard — a leopard he had killed with his bare hands. No man had done it before, and no man has done it since. Ake didn't talk about it often, for it happened long ago, but I had asked him to tell me the story one night while we were smoking our pipes in the museum, looking out the windows at the twinkling lights of Central Park. It had happened in Somaliland on his first trip to Africa, for the Field Museum of Natural History in Chicago, with Dr. D. G. Elliot, in 1896.

"I'd shot a wart hog," he said, "and I went out with a pony boy to bring it to camp. It was almost dark. Just before we reached the carcass, a hyena dashed into the grass with the head of my wart hog in its mouth. That burned me up, because it was a fine specimen. On the way back I saw a shadowy form disappear behind a bush and thought it was another hyena. I fired. Of course, that was a damn fool thing to do. The snarl of a leopard answered. That scared me, for the last thing I wanted was to tangle with a leopard when it was too dark to see the sights of my rifle. Those babies are bad medicine, and don't you forget it. A lion isn't vindictive, but a leopard is a hellcat any time, and when it's wounded it's just a raging, biting, clawing devil. It won't quit until it's dead.

"I wanted to get out of there in a quick way, but the leopard was mad and circled to get behind me. I fired twice, missed, and had an empty rifle. Trying to jam a cartridge into the magazine, I ran and jumped over a bank into a sandy river bed. Just as I shoved the shell in the chamber, 80 pounds of leopard hit me. She knocked the rifle out of my hand and lunged for my throat, but I twisted and she got my right arm in her teeth, way up near the shoulder. My first bullet had broken her foot, thank God, and that saved my life. With one foot injured she couldn't get a purchase in the loose sand; otherwise I'd have been disemboweled in ten seconds by her hind claws.

"I could hear snarling grunts and crunching sounds as she tore my flesh, but I didn't feel any pain. I caught her throat with my left hand and squeezed hard. Her grip loosened a little when I shut off her wind. I tried to pull my arm free. No go. She got another hold farther down. I squeezed again and she gagged. Gradually, I drew my whole arm between her teeth and shoved my hand into her throat. I worked it in as far as I could. Finally, we went down together. We rolled over a couple of times but I got on top. She was on her back, my right fist jammed in her mouth and my left hand clutching her throat. She tried to twist about in the loose sand, but it wouldn't hold.

"I got my knees on her lungs and my elbows in her arm-

[93]

pits, spreading her front legs apart. For a moment we stayed that way, then I thrust down on her breast with my knees. I felt a rib break. She relaxed a little and I gave another surge. Another rib went and blood spilled out of her mouth. The broken bones had pierced her lungs. She was weakening, but so was I. I wondered if I could hold out longer than she could. I put everything I had into a push with both knees. I don't know how long we stayed that way — it seemed like hours — but at last she lay still, only twitching a little. I stood up. Black patches were flickering across my eyes and I felt sick. The pony boy had run away, but he came back when I called and gave me his knife. I stuck it into her breast a couple of times, and she died.

"I was in pretty bad shape when we reached camp. My arm looked like a mass of hamburger and blood oozed through what was left of my clothes. The men were at dinner and when they saw me they got sick. Of course, I was scared of poisoning. All leopard bites are dangerous, because the beasts eat carrion. This one had just been feeding on the hyena I'd shot earlier that day, and her teeth would be particularly foul. After some of the blood was washed off, Dr. Elliot pumped antiseptic into every one of the tooth wounds. There were dozens of them. He gave me so much stuff that as it went in one hole it came out another and before the job was finished I almost wished the leopard had won the fight. But there wasn't a bit of infection."

Akeley's Vision

As we sat around Ake's little office, talking with the sounds of New York's traffic in our ears, Africa seemed so far away as to be part of another world. But I knew it was never very far from Akeley's mind. Since that first trip there, Ake's great aim had been to bring the unknown continent alive for people back home in the cities of the United States. African Hall, the model of which lay before us, was to be the climax of the work that had occupied almost every waking hour of Akeley's life for nearly thirty years. And now, with the backing of wealthy men headed by the multimillionaire founder of the Eastman Kodak Company, the dream was coming true.

Actually, much of it had come true already. Go into any good museum of natural history today and watch the visitors stare in fascination at the lifelike exhibits, listen to the small boys exclaim in wonder at great elephants and the giraffes posed as though eating the leaves of the upper limbs of trees, hear the little girls sigh at the beautifully painted backgrounds and at the baby animals being tended by their mothers. Those are tributes to Carl Akeley. Before Ake's time an elephant in a museum stood foursquare on a pedestal against a blank wall, with very likely an iron rod or two sticking up out of the floor to keep his belly or his trunk from collapsing, and looked less lifelike than a good statue. It was Akeley who brought museum animals to life — and more, for he placed them in accurate representations of their natural backgrounds. If you want to see a live elephant, you can go to a circus or a zoo. But if you want to see the way an elephant lives, you go to a good museum of natural history. And you owe much of what you see there to the genius of Carl Akeley.

It took an incredible combination of rare talents and immense energy to bring this revolution about. Ake started "stuffing" animals where the old-time taxidermists left off, and went on from there to engineering, painting, sculpture and invention. Incidentally, he became one of the greatest big-game hunters who ever fired a gun, though to him hunting was merely a necessary part of his larger work. His life was crammed with adventures. His barehanded battle with the leopard became a classic of hunting-camp talk during his own lifetime, as did the story of the time he was attacked and all but crushed by an elephant, and scores of other experiences of his will be remembered as long as men hunt big game anywhere. Yet Ake did not hunt for sport. "I never shot an animal," he said himself, "unless I needed it for a specimen, or had to shoot it in self-preservation." His goal was something much bigger than a row of trophies, and he had been dedicated to it ever since his boyhood. You couldn't talk with him for five minutes without feeling the power of it.

A bronze plaque now marks the place where Carl Akeley was born, in 1864, on a farm at Clarendon, not far from Rochester, New York. Nobody paid much attention to the event then. Like any farm boy of those days he helped with the work on the place, but every moment he could steal from chores or school was spent in the woods and fields studying birds and animals. They became his most intimate friends. As a young boy he began to experiment with preserving specimens. He borrowed a book on taxidermy and had business cards printed stating that he did "artistic taxidermy in all its branches."

Mounting Jumbo

It was inevitable that Carl should leave the farm and enter the famous Ward's Natural History establishment in Rochester, only 18 miles away. Akeley was 19 years old. Ward's sold natural-history specimens of all kinds, from almost every country of the world, to museums, colleges and laboratories. It was strictly a commercial concern and Akeley was irked beyond measure at the primitive methods used in mounting animals. He wanted to experiment and improve the technique, for even then independence of thought and originality sparked everything he did. But there was little opportunity to show his talents until after he had been at Ward's two years. That year, in 1885, P. T. Barnum's famous circus elephant Jumbo was killed by a railroad locomotive while being led along a narrow right-of-way. Barnum wanted to exhibit the beast mounted, and Professor Ward gave Akeley the assignment. It was a stinking job, literally, for by the time Akeley got there the elephant had lain in blistering sun beside the railway tracks for a day and a half.

With the greatest difficulty Akeley and an assistant kept their "insides in" while removing the skin in sections. Barnum wanted Jumbo to travel with the circus and head the parades, just as he had done when he was the world's most famous living elephant. Moreover, Barnum insisted that the animal be ready for the opening of the circus season in five months. To make the mounted skin light enough to be easily transported and yet strong enough to withstand rain and weather plus inevitable rough treatment were prime requisites. Other taxidermists said it couldn't be done. Akeley figuratively licked his chops; that was just the sort of problem he liked. He constructed a manikin of planks and oak crosspieces, fastened together with iron plates. Over this outline skeleton, narrow strips of basswood, steamed to bend easily, simulated the flesh and gave a base for the skin, which was tacked to the wood. It was an excellent job and set a new standard for large-animal taxidermy. Jumbo was ready on time, and traveled with the circus for many years. He finally found a home in Tufts College in Medford, Massachusetts. His skeleton stands today in the American Museum of Natural History.

Akeley remained at Ward's for another year, and then went to Milwaukee at the invitation of his friend and companion, the brilliant scientist William Morton Wheeler. One of the plans of his youth had been to enter the Yale Scientific School, but another dream had been growing in him — one from which he never deviated — to make taxidermy a real art; and he came to realize that academic life was not for him. He experimented with small habitat exhibits, depicting animals in their natural surroundings in grass, flowers and foliage. A muskrat group done for the Milwaukee Museum was the first to use a painted background and accompanying vegetation to demonstrate in museum exhibition ecology, the functional relation between an animal and the environment in which it lives.

In 1894, after eight years in Milwaukee, when he was 30 years old, Carl received an invitation from Sir William Flower, Director of the British Museum of Natural History, to come to London and take charge of their Department of Preparation. It was a great opportunity, but en route to England he stopped at the newly born Field

Museum in Chicago. There, Dr. D. G. Elliot offered him the contract for preparing exhibits of mammals. Akeley abandoned his London plans and started at once on his new task. Two years later he sailed for Africa with Dr. Elliot on his first expedition to the country that became his great love.

Akeley was in the seventh heaven of delight, for at last he would be able to observe the animals he was to mount in the wild; he would have the chance to skin and study the anatomy of freshly killed specimens, and photograph and measure them himself. Without that personal observation, he was convinced, no man could approach the standards he visualized for the future of taxidermy.

It was on this expedition that he had the experience with the leopard. His superb strength and vitality brought him back to normal in a surprisingly short time.

Ake took each new experience, including that one, to heart, thought about it, and made its lesson a part of his knowledge of the wild. Every day his respect and affection for animals increased, and he seemed able to understand their psychology, to enter into their minds and anticipate their thoughts, as only one who really loves them can do. That was why he became such a phenomenal hunter.

African Adventures

This first expedition dedicated Akeley to Africa and his life's work. In the so-called Dark Continent he found an abundance of game such as it was in primeval days. He found natives who had never seen a white man, animals that lived their lives in a wholly primitive world.

Until the day of his death, Akeley kept a fresh mind. It

was incredibly sensitive to new impressions, never shaded by preconceptions. He approached every experience and every creature, animal or human, with an absolutely open attitude. That person, or that animal, sold itself to him on its merits alone. He became fascinated with elephants because he found in them loyalty, affection, intelligence and unbelievable cunning. He never liked the sneaking, vindictive, carrion-eating leopards. For lions, he conceived a profound admiration. Rhinos gave him a great laugh. They are such awkward, blundering brutes that he had difficulty in taking them seriously. He had been warned they were among the most dangerous of all game; they were big, they charged on the slightest provocation, and if one got you it was a through ticket to the grave. The only way to handle them was to shoot and take no chances. But Akeley subsequently discovered that when it comes to brain power a rhino simply isn't there. He does have a certain amount of gray matter within his great saddle-shaped skull, but it might as well not be there at all so far as use of it is concerned. His nose seems to be the only one of his five senses that works even subnormally. When he smells something, he charges wildly about, first in one direction, then in another, with no clear objective. If he loses the scent and his little piglike nearsighted eyes can't pick up a cause for the odor, he apparently forgets what he started out to do and goes quietly to sleep.

A Lion Is a Gentleman

Lions sold themselves to Akeley immediately. He often said, "The lion is a great gentleman. He has dignity, reserve, and pride. He kills for food, never wantonly. Although slow to anger, when once offended, he is terrible in retribution. But he is not vindictive. His courage is phenomenal."

Akeley had never seen a lion outside a cage when he went to Somaliland, and his first encounter gave him the fright of his life. He had been hunting oryx, and was just about to mount his pony, when two lions and a lioness walked across a stretch of sand right in the open, not a hundred yards away. Three lions seemed a pretty large order, for he was alone and had never tangled with a lion. He sent his gun boys on the ponies to circle them and they went into a nearby patch of jungle. Just outside the edge, Akeley waited. Suddenly, with a terrific roar, the lioness burst out of the bush in mid-air, springing diagonally away from him. She saw him instantly, twisted, and landed facing him only a few feet away. Just as he fired, a lion jumped over her back. That disconcerted him and his shot only wounded her. For some reason, instead of charging, she turned and followed the lion into the cover.

Ake was pretty close to death in that instant. Had the lioness seen him before she leaped out of the bush, she would have landed squarely on his head. Her great claws and teeth would have crushed his skull like an eggshell. Ake was badly shaken, but he wasn't ready to quit. He wanted at least one of the lions. The boys set fire to the cover but the two lions escaped on the opposite side. The lioness didn't appear. Evidently she had been fatally wounded by his first shot.

Not infrequently lions will keep on going if they miss their initial spring.

I saw it happen in a motion picture brought back by

[101]

Lady Grace McKenzie. Without doubt, it is the most amazing movie ever taken of a charging lion.

She had wounded a lion which lay up in a patch of grass in plain sight, growling and switching its tail. They knew the beast would charge at any moment. The photographer set up his camera, with Lady McKenzie on his left, and their white hunter somewhat in front at the right. Suddenly, the lion leaped out, coming straight for them in tremendous bounds. The woman fired, but the beast never faltered. The white hunter's gun roared when the lion was almost at them. Still it came on. The man turned to run, tripped, and fell flat on his face. The lion leaped right over him, brushing the camera as it passed, and kept on. It fell dead just inside a patch of jungle. All of them were petrified with fright. When they had recovered enough to speak, the photographer moaned, "If only I had got that picture. There'll never be another chance like it."

Lady McKenzie gasped, "I think you did get it. Your face was at the view finder and I'm sure you were grinding all the time."

"If I did, it was automatic. I don't remember a thing. I was too damned scared."

When he developed the film, there was the whole story. The start of the charge, the lion looming larger and larger in the picture, then Lady McKenzie's shot. You see the white hunter shoot, turn, fall, and the lion pass over him. That film never will be duplicated except by chance. It brought the audience right up on their feet.

Akeley maintained that nine times out of ten a lion will let you alone if you don't bother him, but you can't annoy him beyond a certain point. He is a peaceful citizen, believing in the motto "Live and let live." But when his dignity is offended nothing will stop him, and his courage is superb.

Akeley, who always stood on the side of the beasts, believed that, except in a very few instances, lions only become habitual man-eaters when they are old or sick, and unable to kill game for food. Then they raid the native villages, feeding on domestic herds, and sometimes humans, to keep from starving. But this is not always so. The classic example of man-eaters is the group of young, healthy lions that stopped construction on a part of the Uganda railroad. When the railroad was being built, thousands of native workers were employed, and many died. Foolishly enough, their bodies were put in the brush unburied. Lions found them and thus acquired a taste for human flesh. They began to hunt men, just as they would hunt any other game. I have forgotten how many natives they accounted for, but the toll ran into scores. A Colonel J. H. Patterson was sent to clear them out. He had some amazing experiences, which he recounted in a book called *Man-eaters of Tsavo*. Akeley and I were at a dinner of the Explorers Club the night Colonel Patterson told his story. It sounded like a movie thriller.

New Methods of Taxidermy

When Akeley returned to Chicago after the 1896 Somaliland expedition, he was appointed head of the Department of Preparation in the rapidly growing Field Museum. He was in the full vigor of middle life, a man of medium height, large head and powerful shoulders. Although his face was habitually set in rather grim lines, it could break into a quick, warm smile when he saw a friend. One felt, instinctively, that his life was dedicated to a serious purpose; that time was running out and brooked no delay; that there were too few hours of the day to do what must be done. Sleep was a necessary evil, only to be indulged in when his exhausted body cried out insistently for rest. New discoveries in technique came so rapidly that some were abandoned almost as soon as they had been put into practice, but each opened a wider vista of museum exhibition. With his passion for perfection, Akeley was never satisfied. His goal was so high that it outran the imagination of those who were responsible for the museum. At times they became impatient when they saw the results of work that was far superior to anything else in the world, and wished he would at least hesitate in his ambitious race for perfection. But he would never compromise with his ideals. To their everlasting credit, be it said that the authorities of the museum realized they had discovered an outstanding genius and did their best to give him a free rein.

It would be tedious to detail the steps by which Akeley took taxidermy out of the realm of "stuffing" into that of true art. Briefly, this is what happened. When Akeley first came to Ward's, the "upholsterer" method of putting irons through an animal's legs fastened to a board in the body, and then cramming the relaxed skin with as much stuffing as it would hold, had been generally abandoned in favor of a clay-covered manikin. The body was roughly outlined in excelsior, covered with wet clay, the skin adjusted and the face and head modeled to a semblance of its natural appearance. It was a pretty poor method. When the clay dried, the skin cracked and shrank and the beast looked like a caricature of its former self.

The next forward step was to model an animal full size in clay, exactly as a sculptor does, working out the most minute details of anatomy from dozens of measurements, photographs, sketches and careful studies of every muscle. Then Akeley cast the model in plaster and, from the mold, constructed a light hollow manikin that perfectly reproduced the clay original; on this the skin was adjusted.

Akeley's methods completely revolutionized the mounting of large specimens. Today, their results are seen in every modern museum in the world, for not only did he publicize each step of his experiments but men came to him for instruction, and followed his technique even when they could not study under him personally.

James L. Clark was his star pupil. Dr. Hermon Bumpus, at that time director of the American Museum of Natural History, was deeply impressed with Akeley's work. Dr. Bumpus had recently employed Clark, a young artist from Providence, Rhode Island, in the taxidermy department. He asked Akeley if he would teach Clark his methods. Ake was glad to do so, and Jim spent some months with him in Chicago. Eventually, they went to Africa together on an elephant hunt. Much later, it fell to Clark's lot to direct the completion of the African Hall after Akeley's death.

While he was with the Field Museum, Carl married a charming, quiet woman who merged her life completely into his, and who later accompanied him on several trips to Africa. At their comfortable home in Chicago, and later in New York, Delia Akeley (her friends all called her Mickey) was a gracious hostess who managed the social side of their

life with unusual efficiency and tact. In Africa she soon became equally efficient as a field assistant to her husband, and
developed into a fine shot. On one of their trips she shot an
elephant which was said to be the biggest ever taken
in Africa.

The Fascinating Elephant

Ever since his Jumbo experience, Akeley had thought of
elephants. Perhaps it was their majestic size, great strength
and almost human intelligence that awakened his admiration and respect. He always wanted to see and study them
in their jungle homes, and when, in 1906, the Field Museum
again sent him to British East Africa especially to collect a
group of elephants he was as excited as a child.

He discovered that elephants are extremely difficult to
study. One might suppose that so large an animal would be
easy to see at a long distance. Nothing could be a greater
fallacy. Its dark body harmonizes perfectly with the lights
and shadows of the jungle; when an elephant is standing
motionless, a man can almost run into it without knowing
it is there. Moreover, the huge beast can move through the
thickest tangle as noiselessly as a cat on a soft rug. Akeley
tells of being so close to an old cow in a dense forest that he
could hear the rumbling of her stomach, and yet when she
realized he was near the rumbling ceased, as it always does
when they are suspicious, and she left without his hearing a
sound.

I asked Akeley about the romantic idea that elephants
go to a certain spot to die. He didn't take much stock in the
"graveyards." He did say that several reliable sportsmen had

reported finding numbers of skeletons and bones near certain pools in the jungle, but he believed that could be explained in other ways. For instance, natives often shoot poisoned darts into elephants. These do not kill immediately. They induce a great craving for water. The animals will go to the nearest water hole and not leave until they either die or recover. Few if any elephants dead of natural causes are found in the forests. He thought this was because when ill they seek the deepest solitudes and die there alone. Eventually, the decomposing carcass brings hyenas, leopards, jackals and other scavengers, and every scrap of meat is devoured. The luxuriant jungle growth soon hides the bones that have not been carried away. Many elephants die in swamps where the remains sink in the mud.

There is a perennial dispute among African sportsmen as to whether elephants, lions or buffalos are the most dangerous of the big game. I know Akeley favored elephants — and not only because he had been mauled by one. He often said that if a man continues to hunt elephants persistently he will inevitably be killed or narrowly escape death. Friends who hunted with Ake told me that nobody more careful ever shot in Africa, and yet an elephant got him.

It happened high up on the slopes of Mount Kenya. Akeley had been following the spoor of three big bulls and early in the morning caught up with them in a bamboo jungle.

While he was standing with the rifle leaning against his body, one of the bulls suddenly charged him. The safety catch on his rifle jammed but he swung in between the tusks as the elephant forced him down. The tightly curled trunk pressed against his chest. It broke most of his ribs and he blacked out. By some miracle one of the tusks struck a rock or a root, which prevented the animal from crushing Akeley to a jelly. The elephant pulled back and saw the gun boy and porters running away. He left Carl and started after them. The natives scattered like a covey of quail and none were caught.

Ake lay all night in the freezing cold, for the porters thought he was dead and they would not touch him. At last he became conscious and the natives brought him into their tent. A messenger had been sent to Mrs. Akeley, but she did not arrive until after daybreak.

Mickey told me that Carl was a dreadful sight. The elephant's trunk had scalped his forehead, closed one eye, smashed his nose and torn open one cheek so that it hung down and exposed his teeth in a horrible grin. Many of his ribs were broken. Several had punctured his lungs and blood was running out of the corners of his mouth. She knew what that meant and it scared her worst of all. A Scotch medical missionary finally reached him. The doctor's skill saved his life.

But in spite of the fact that the elephant is such a formidable fighter, Akeley always maintained that if it were not molested it wanted only to carry on its family life like any other peaceful citizen of the jungle. Its sagacity, versatility, and a certain comradeship were the characteristics that made the animal so fascinating to him.

The Cement Gun

When Akeley mounted the elephants for the Field Museum, he employed an entirely new method, which, incidentally, resulted in one of his most successful inventions, the cement gun. The museum, at that time, occupied the old Art Building of the World's Columbian Exposition. It was poorly constructed of stuccoed brick, and the walls were peeling alarmingly. Contractors asked a prohibitive price to repair the damage. As usual when any extraordinary problem arose, no matter what its nature, Akeley was called in for consultation. He had been using a big, handmade atomizer operated by compressed air to squirt liquid plaster under the skin of an elephant after it was on the manikins. Why not, he thought, use a machine that would spray a very liquid cement on the side of the building, mixing it in the nozzle of the hose? There was nothing of the kind on the market, so he designed and built an apparatus himself. I went to visit Akeley in Chicago at that time, and found him supervising workmen on rehabilitating the old museum walls.

It seemed a far cry from mounting animals in his studio, but no one was ever surprised at what Akeley did.

The invention proved so successful that he and Dewey, his assistant, set to work to improve the original model. After two years it was perfected, patents obtained and the Cement Gun Company organized. The gun has been used widely at home and abroad, on the Panama Canal, on the cement ships during World War I and on the roofs of mines, buildings, irrigation ditches, tunnels and reservoirs. In 1916, the Franklin Institute for the Promotion of the Mechanical Arts awarded its John Scott Legacy Medal to Carl Akeley for his invention of the cement gun.

In Africa, when he was convalescing from blackwater fever, he watched a native woman milking a goat. To amuse himself, he designed a milking machine which proved eminently successful.

During the thirteen years that Akeley was with the Field Museum he had conceived two great halls. One was to be devoted to Illinois Birds and the other to North American Ruminants and Fur Bearers. But his loyal supporter, President Marshall Field, died and the proposed new halls went into the discard. Ake felt that he had served his time with the Field Museum and, about 1908, suggested to Director Bumpus that he go to Africa to collect an elephant group for the American Museum of Natural History in New York. His plan was accepted, and Ake prepared for the expedition. This ended his official connection with the Field Museum. The Akeleys moved to New York in 1909.

A short time earlier, Theodore Roosevelt, then President of the United States, asked Congressman Mann to bring Akeley to the White House. At dinner, Roosevelt told Akeley he intended to go to Alaska for a hunt when he left Washington. But before the evening ended, the President had become so interested in Akeley's stories of Africa, that he decided to go there instead and collect for the Smithsonian Institution.

In Africa with Roosevelt

At that dinner Akeley related an incident about when sixteen lions came out of a cave on the MacMillan estate in Africa. Roosevelt, who was having trouble with a refractory Senate, chuckled and turned to Congressman Mann, his voice breaking into its high falsetto: "I'd like to have those lions right here in Washington today," he said.

"What would you do with them, Mr. President?" Mann asked. "I'd turn them loose in the Senate." "But aren't you afraid they'd make some mistakes?" "Not if they stayed long enough," the President laughed. The story got around. Later, when Roosevelt started for Africa, the Senate retaliated with the slogan "America expects every lion to do his duty."

During the planning of the Roosevelt African Expedition, Akeley was often at the White House, and he fell under the Colonel's magic charm, as did all of us who knew him intimately. Roosevelt wanted Ake to accompany him, but Ake was committed to getting the elephant group for the American Museum of Natural History and did not see how their two expeditions could merge. They planned to meet in Africa, however, and Ake suggested that Colonel Roosevelt shoot at least one of the specimens for the group, which would include cows, calves and bulls.

Carl's old friend Jimmy Clark had been in Africa for nine months when Ake left New York in 1909, and Clark joined Akeley as an assistant. They overtook the Roosevelt safari and, leaving Jim in his camp, Ake spent the night with the Colonel, whose party had seen elephants that day. The next morning eight cows and calves were discovered having a nap under an acacia tree. The men watched them from behind an anthill, and Akeley pointed out a cow he thought would do for the group.

He expected Roosevelt to shoot from where he stood, but instead, the Colonel walked out straight toward the elephants. Akeley wasn't at all happy, because he knew the danger, but there was nothing for it except to follow with Kermit Roosevelt, the Colonel's son.

[111]

Halfway across the open space, the cow spread her ears, curled her trunk and charged with an angry squeal. Roosevelt shot and the elephant went to her knees, but got up. The whole herd came on bellowing and screaming. The Colonel fired again and the cow went down for good, but the others didn't hesitate. Akeley and Kermit had to shoot to turn the herd. They succeeded in turning it just in time, but killed two more elephants in doing it. The men would have been annihilated if the remaining animals had pushed their charge home.

Akeley was faced with the tremendous task of skinning the three elephants before they spoiled under the blazing sun. He sent word to Clark, at his own camp, to come at once with men and salt to preserve the hides. Clark started out with a black boy as a guide, but lost his way. Jim was frantic, for he knew how much Akeley needed assistance, and began firing his rifle. At last he heard answering shots. Following them to the Roosevelt safari, he found Kermit, who gave him two other guides. They, too, got lost. Clark had to spend a night in the open, but the next morning he encountered Colonel Roosevelt returning to his camp. Under the guidance of the Colonel's boys, Clark finally found Akeley.

Jim was amazed when he saw that Carl had the skins off all three elephants. He had done it by working frantically the entire night and pushing his natives to the limit of their endurance. Even then, they almost lost the specimens, plus their own lives. Fires, kindled by natives some distance away to give their flocks fresh grass in the spring, swept down upon the camp, fanned by a strong wind. Only by lighting backfires and fighting furiously did they keep from being encircled and roasted alive. Some of the natives were badly burned. Clark and Akeley emerged as black as chimney sweeps and ready to drop from exhaustion.

Handling a Dead Elephant

To handle a dead elephant in the field is a tremendous undertaking, especially when it must be done with the care which Akeley demanded. The usual broiling sun, added to the gases of decomposition, will cause the epidermis to "slip" in a few hours. Akeley's procedure was to erect a tarpaulin over the carcass and keep natives constantly bathing the skin with strong salt solution. The hide was removed in four sections, first from one side, then from the other. When it was off, the work had only begun. The skin is two and one half inches thick, and it must be pared down with small knives until it is thin enough to assimilate the preserving salt. But salt will absorb moisture, and moisture is fatal. Akeley solved that problem by having his boys collect honeycombs from the numerous bee trees and extract the beeswax. Then he coated cotton cloth with the wax, and wrapped up the salted and dried skins in bundles that would be waterproof.

The killing of the big bull for the American Museum group was dramatic for, after the elephant was wounded, it started to hunt the hunter and Ake was saved only by a lucky break. He had come upon a herd of elephants in very thick jungle. Through an opening he saw a tusk on a dark mass which, at first, he thought was a gigantic boulder. It was a big tusk — a very big tusk. Then he made out the other. Both were perfect. That was the bull he wanted for the group, an elephant that would be a worthy representative of the largest animal in the world in the greatest museum.

Akeley had to calculate where the brain would be, for he couldn't see the eye. When he fired, all hell broke loose in the forest as the herd stampeded. The bull dropped, but recovered and went off by himself. For two hours, Ake and his gunbearer followed the trail. Suddenly, with absolutely no warning, the elephant dashed out of the bush directly across their path, not fifteen feet away. Had the charge been straight at them they could never have escaped, but in the thick forest the beast couldn't see the men and had to rely on scent or sound. Obviously, it had become tired of being followed and had doubled back on its tracks to await its pursuers. Akeley fired two quick shots. The elephant went on for a short distance, and then stopped again. Ake could hear it grumbling and thought it would be down for good in a short time, so he waited. In a little while the elephant got his wind, squealed, and charged again. It couldn't make the grade. It crashed headlong into the jungle, and the bull he had searched Africa for two years to find was dead.

When it came to mounting the elephant in New York, Akeley characteristically developed a completely new method, as superior to the technique he had used in preparing the Field Museum specimens as they were over his original Jumbo. In the first place, it was all-important that the skin itself should be almost as soft as glove leather. He had experimented with tanning solutions for years, and at last developed a formula that met his exacting standards. It required twelve weeks of daily work and manipulation to prepare the skin for mounting. During that time it was pared down with the greatest care until the hide emerged as beautiful leather less than one-quarter inch in thickness, and uniform throughout its vast expanse.

Akeley's method is too complicated to be explained in detail, but fundamentally it consisted of building the manikin on the *inside* of the elephant's skin while it lay in the plaster mold, instead of completing the manikin and putting the skin over it. Again he had revolutionized the methods of mounting large pachyderms.

It may seem that I use the word "revolutionize" carelessly. I assure you I do not. It is a statement of fact. The whole museum world followed Akeley's methods, step by step. He was completely unselfish. Each time his experiments produced a new or better technique in any department of preparation to which he directed his genius, it had the widest possible circulation among those who could profit by the knowledge. He often went at personal sacrifice of time and strength to museum association meetings, to explain with lantern slides and exhibits what a new process could accomplish and how to do it.

Whenever he mounted an animal, he made a small model in clay, working out the pose, anatomy and expression in the most minute detail. These were finished statuettes, beautiful in design and execution, and often inspiring. His friends urged him to give them permanence in bronze. Other artists assured him they would find a ready market. But Ake refused. It was not until the vision of African Hall had taken firm root in his mind that he realized that sculpture might be a means to achieve the culmination of his life's work. Through it, he could demonstrate the artis-

tic possibilities of taxidermy, or at least show that a taxi-
dermist could be an artist. Also, he believed that if he did a
bronze, it should tell a definite story of the animals he loved.

Elephants dominated his mind at this time. It was natural, therefore, that he should choose for his first sculpture an incident that showed the strong fraternal feeling
of the animals. He had never forgotten the time when he
tried a heart shot at a big bull. Always before, he had killed
his elephants with a bullet in the brain, but the head of this
particular animal was obscured. The heart is eighteen or
twenty inches long and about a foot in diameter; not a difficult mark if you can guess its location accurately. Ake
fired at the heart with both barrels and then grabbed his
other rifle from the gun boy. He expected the herd to
charge, but instead they made off in the other direction.
Ake climbed an anthill and saw an amazing performance.
The bull was down on its side. Around him were ten
or twelve other elephants trying desperately, with their
trunks and tusks, to get him on his feet. They moved his
great bulk fifteen or twenty yards in their efforts, but
couldn't get him up. Their leader was dead.

The Wounded Comrade

Later, a Major Harrison told him that in the Congo he
came upon four elephants. He killed one and knocked another down. Immediately, the two survivors helped the
wounded animal to its feet, and supporting him on either
side, moved off into the forest. These incidents inspired
Akeley to do his first, and most famous, bronze, entitled
The Wounded Comrade. It shows two bull elephants half

carrying between them an injured companion which can just maintain its feet. When the bronze arrived, Ake telephoned my office and asked me to come down to his studio on the second floor of the museum. It was almost five o'clock and the lights of Central Park were winking on like stars in a dark sky. The bronze stood on a table. Ake was sitting slumped in his chair smoking his pipe.

"There it is, Roy," he said, "what do you think of it?"

To me it seemed superb, and I said so. "Yes, but you aren't a sculptor. Phimister Proctor is coming up in a short time. To my mind, he is one of the best American animal sculptors of the present generation. Proctor is honest. He'll tell me what he really thinks. It's damned important."

Proctor arrived, and as he walked into the studio his eyes caught *The Wounded Comrade* on a modeling pedestal. He only said, "Hello," to us, and stood studying the bronze for a long time. Finally, he burst out, "Ake, it's magnificent. I wish to God I had done it."

Carl said huskily, "I'm glad you like it. Let's have a drink."

How much Proctor thought of it was shown later when his friend George D. Pratt ordered the first copy without ever having seen the original. *The Wounded Comrade* won immediate and almost lyrical commendation from art critics. Akeley was elected to the American Sculpture Society, and that pleased him. A copy of the statue went to Theodore Roosevelt. It stood on the desk of his study at Sagamore Hill, Oyster Bay, Long Island.

"That," the Colonel said to me one day, "is the finest tribute to a noble animal ever put in sculpture. Only Akeley could have done it."

In the next years, Carl did other bronzes, each telling a

story of African life. All of them were successful and he achieved the reputation of being one of the foremost animal sculptors of his time.

Akeley did not lead a balanced existence. He had no hours of play, as the ordinary man conceives it. The particular problem on which he was working at the moment seemed to occupy his mind so completely that he could relegate it to the subconscious background for only a short time. His social life centered about friends with mutual interests, and the conversation inevitably drifted to sculpture, photography, invention, museum exhibition, shooting or natural history. I never knew him to sit down to a hand of cards; he had no small talk. Hostesses who tried to capture him as the star around whom they could build a dinner were doomed to disappointment unless he knew the evening would include someone whom he might interest in his work. He and his wife lived modestly but comfortably in an apartment a few blocks from the museum.

Like almost every explorer, Ake had to raise the money for his expeditions through private donations. The idea that a museum provides all the funds, and sends a man on an expedition with nothing to do but carry on the field work, could not be more fallacious. This happens in small trips, like routine departmental investigations, but not in big projects. Those must be financed by the originator himself. The museum gives its blessing and backing, contributes men from its staff and sometimes a modest amount of money, but that is about as far as it can go on its budget. Even the worst hardships of field work are pure pleasure compared to the job of raising the funds that make it possible.

Inevitably Akeley, like all the rest of us, had to eat a good many unwanted dinners and be the center of attraction at some boring functions, but he cut them to the minimum. He did most of his entertaining in his museum studio; there he was a fascinating host and it was a rare privilege to be an invited guest.

Ake had a wide acquaintance, including many great of the world. Whether it was a prince of the realm or a little-known artist, he received them in the same costume: clay-spotted trousers, open shirt, coatless, with a pipe always in his hand. The Duke of Connaught came one day by appointment, but Ake was in his usual working clothes and treated him exactly as he would anyone else. The duke, I may say, was fascinated by his personality. Some men, like C. F. Kettering, Orville Wright, and Gifford Pinchot became close friends because they had mutual interests and great admiration for Akeley's genius.

When absorbed in some particular problem, Carl lived a life remote from material things. But even under great stress he was always kind and considerate and never lost the gentleness that made people love him.

Akeley was indifferent to money except insofar as it would enable him to do his work. He hated lecturing, but he did a good deal of it because it gave him the wherewithal to finance his projects. His lectures were as casual and informal as the man himself. He simply went out on the platform and told stories of his fantastic life just as though he were talking to a few friends in his home or studio. Of course, it made a tremendous hit. In five minutes his personality could capture any audience.

Another chapter in Carl Akeley's life was brought about by his interest in photography. Not only was it important to his work, but it would help preserve a record of the already vanishing animals and native customs of Africa. When he was searching for the great bull elephant for the American Museum group, he obtained what is still the most remarkable close-up photograph of a charging elephant ever made. Jim Clark was with him to act as "cover man" with a rifle, while Ake used the camera. They came upon three cow elephants and a calf. As Akeley got his camera ready, the cow winded them and charged at full speed. Jim was determined to wait until he heard the camera shutter click, but it took all the nerve he had not to squeeze the trigger of his rifle. The elephant loomed bigger and bigger, ears spread, trunk curled, coming like an express train straight for them. When the image almost filled the view finder, Ake pressed the button and Clark fired instantly. He turned the cow, but it took bullets from two other men, who had arrived from behind them, to drop the beast. Akeley had absolute confidence in Clark for he knew his courage, and, with his face jammed into the hood of the reflex camera, he was so absorbed in watching the image enlarge on the ground glass that he was completely oblivious to danger.

Even after he and Jimmy had risked their lives for the photo, Ake nearly lost it. In those days we all used glass plates, as films were in their infancy. While developing that night, Carl became so excited that he dropped and broke the plate. It was retouched, however, and a new negative made.

Lion Spearing

Akeley was continually irritated by the limitations of
the existing cameras, particularly those taking motion pictures. An expedition to the Uasin Gishu plateau, to obtain
movies of the spectacular lion spearing by Nandi natives,
disappointed him bitterly. He had gathered a hundred
Nandi spearmen at a government station, and during the
first morning, they saw an animal go into a patch of cover.
Ake set up his camera, hoping that the supposed lion would
be driven into the open, where he could photograph it as
the spears were thrown. But the operation did not proceed
as planned. The spearmen entered the bush from all sides
but, instead of a lion's roar, the angry growl of a leopard
sounded above the shouts. Then pandemonium broke loose.
A few seconds later two of the boys came out of the
thicket, carrying a third. His scalp hung down over his face
in a bloody mass, and his shoulder had a dozen gashes from
the ripping claws. Behind them came a group of Nandi
carrying the dead leopard. Its skin showed sixty spear holes.

Akeley took the boy into the shade of a mimosa tree and
sewed his scalp back in place. The native made no comment,
except to ask what was going on. The next morning he objected strenuously to being sent back out of action. His
wounds didn't seem to bother him and he wanted to continue with the others.

A few days later, the party saw several lions come out
of the grass and disappear in thick bush. The spearmen
surrounded the cover and the lions tried to escape, but no
matter where they charged a native bobbed up in front of
them. It takes a good bit of courage to meet the rush of an

[121]

angry lion singlehanded with only a spear and a shield, but the Nandi never hesitated. The fight ended with three dead lions — but no picture! The camera was too cumbersome and could not be swung about quickly enough to record the action.

At last, Akeley did get a picture of sorts, and witnessed a furious battle between a single spearman and a lioness. The native stumbled on the beast in the grass, and the two fought it out hand to claw. When the others arrived, the Nandi was on his back protecting himself with his shield, a single bite in his leg, while the lioness lay dying beside him.

What finally decided Akeley not to return to Africa without a proper camera happened when the spearmen brought a lion to bay in the open on top of a hill. Unfortunately, the boys were too eager, and before Ake could set up his camera, speared the lion, in full sunlight. "I think it was the most hearthbreaking failure I ever had," he said. "I intended never to have another, and from that minute I began working on a camera that takes no time to adjust. I got it, finally, but that one moment of poignant disappointment cost me many months of toil."

It was characteristic of Akeley to design and make his own motion-picture camera if there was none on the market which would produce the results he desired. Before he reached New York, the plans were clear in his mind. All other cameras were square; his would be round, thus saving weight and space. Why use a square box when you are dealing with a roll of film? The camera must be movable diagonally, up and down, from side to side, and easy to aim instantly in any direction. The shutter must admit the maximum light, for that is all-important when photographing in jungle. Also, it must have facilities for instant attachment of telephoto lenses. These were the basic requirements.

The Akeley Camera

All Akeley needed when he returned to the American Museum was a sponsor, and I helped him there. A young friend of mine, M. S. (Ted) Slocum, who had recently graduated from Princeton with an engineering degree, no experience, but considerable money, met Akeley at my house. He was infected with Ake's enthusiasm and decided to finance the camera's manufacture. I warned him he was in for a rich experience if his money held out, but he must understand that Akeley would settle for nothing but a perfect product. Nevertheless, he went ahead.

Akeley rented a loft not far from the museum, installed machinery and persuaded Jimmy Clark to enter upon the venture with him. They designed a camera infinitely better than anything on the market, but during its production, at least a dozen new ideas developed in Ake's fertile mind to improve on the original model. Immediately he scrapped the whole thing. He planned a quite different, and better, machine, and again they started to manufacture. But in the meantime, Ake had dreamed up other gadgets that would do still more. The second model was scrapped.

This went on for months. With Akeley's passion for perfection, he would not consent to put a camera on the market that did not satisfy him to the ultimate degree.

[123   ]

Ted Slocum was in a swivet. He had poured thousands of dollars into the work, only to see it go into the discard. At last, he reached his limit. He still maintained his faith in the camera and his affection for Ake, but he had gone as far as he could. Regretfully, he had to call it quits. Even though his friends bought stock in the Akeley Camera Company up to the limit of their ability, Ake was backed up against the wall. He faced the end of all his work just when a really perfect model was in sight. Then some wealthy Cleveland men formed a syndicate to refinance the camera. As far as I know, Ake got very little out of his two years of heart-breaking work except the John Wetherill Medal from the Franklin Institute, and the satisfaction of a job well done. Now he could go to Africa and not miss lion spearing, or any other picture, for lack of proper equipment. To him that was remuneration enough. The cameras were subsequently used by all the big field expeditions in many parts of the world, and by newsreel photographers; for years, anywhere that fast action had to be recorded on film, the Akeley camera was supreme.

About the time the camera was finished, the United States entered World War I, and all normal activities ceased. The government ordered a number of the cameras and Akeley accepted a contract whereby the entire output of the shop went to the War Department. It was used with great success at the fighting front.

War Service

Akeley, of course, was keen to do his bit in the war and became a specialist on mechanical devices and optical equipment in the Division of Research of the Engineer Corps. Whenever a problem, mechanical or otherwise, arose he went to look things over, and if he had suggestions to make, he was assigned to that job. Among other things, he developed a device for searchlight control which was eventually patented by the government in his name. He was offered a major's commission but preferred to remain out of khaki.

He probably declined a commission for the same reason that he would never accept a salary from the American Museum of Natural History. Not that he had an independent income — or, in fact, much money at all most of the time — but if he'd been on salary he would have felt constrained to abide by the museum's rules. These were benign and elastic, and few of us ever had any trouble operating well within them; but they were still rules, and Ake was not a man who could stand being bound in the slightest degree. All the years he was with the museum he was paid a "retaining fee," which for purposes of ready cash was the same as a salary, but which allowed him the freedom of an independent agent, to devote himself to whatever he wished to do, whether it came within the museum's usual scope or not.

During the war he worked for the army engineers on an arrangement calling for pay of $10 a day, without expense money; it did not even defray his railway fares. But fortunately, the museum had continued to pay him his "retaining fee" during his war service. All his savings had been poured into the camera long ago. Though many things captured Ake's interest at one time or another during his busy and varied life, money was never one of them.

After the war ended, Akeley again began to dream his

dreams. While convalescing from being mauled by the bull elephant, he had visualized a great African Hall for the American Museum of Natural History; a hall which would bring not only the animals of the Dark Continent but *actual parts* of Africa to the people of America and the world.

"African Hall," he wrote, "will tell the story of jungle peace; a story that is sincere and faithful to the African beasts as I have known them, and it will, I hope, tell that story so convincingly that the traditions of jungle horrors and impenetrable forests may be obliterated."

The vision became the dominating passion of Akeley's life. It was to be the culmination of his years of work and experimentation in museum exhibition. He first presented the idea to President Henry Fairfield Osborn and the American Museum trustees in 1911. It was accepted for immediate execution, and mounting the elephant group got under way but, like so many other things, became dormant for the duration of World War I. It came to life again in 1920, and Akeley set about gathering the material in the field.

Gorillas headed his list. The great ape was one of the least-known large animals in the world. Most of the information rested on the account of the Frenchman Paul De Chaillu, who, in 1855, was the first white man to kill a gorilla. He pictures the animal as of "immense body, huge chest, great muscular arms, fiercely glaring deep gray eyes, a hellish expression of face like some nightmare vision and a strange discordant half-human cry." He recounts the superstition that these "wild men of the woods" capture native women and carry them away to be raped at leisure. The sculptor Fremiet, using this idea, made a life-sized bronze statue of a huge gorilla carrying a half-naked girl, obviously a French

[126   ]

model, under its arm. The ape's face wears a fiendish expression of anticipatory pleasure. Some well-meaning person, I have forgotten who, presented this enormous bronze to the American Museum of Natural History. Of course, it could not be exhibited there, and for many years it reposed in the basement near the elevator. It used to burn up Akeley. "Why in hell," he would say, "should a good sculptor waste his talents reproducing a lie? The whole thing is absurd."

Although Ake had never seen a wild gorilla, he was convinced that most of the stories told about its ferocity and bad temper were false. Judging by his long experience with other dangerous animals, he believed that he would find the gorilla to be a perfectly amiable and decent creature; if it attacks man, that is because it thinks it is being attacked itself; then it doubtless would fight to the finish, using every ounce of its strength and teeth against its adversary. So Akeley was predisposed in the gorilla's favor, and quite certain that it was a much maligned beast. This was a perfectly natural attitude, for he looked upon most animals as friends. Moreover, he had kept a small monkey as a pet in his apartment for years, and loved it devotedly. It was named J.T., after John T. McCutcheon, the famous cartoonist of the *Chicago Tribune*, who had been with him in Africa when the baby was captured. In a way, J.T. took the place of a child to him, for Ake never had any children.

Not only did Carl want to obtain specimens and studies of gorillas for the African Hall, but motion pictures as well. For the first time, he would use in the field the Akeley camera on which he had labored so long. Also, no photographs or movies of wild gorillas had ever been taken. He told me that he had never looked forward to an expedition with such keen anticipation.

To Africa for Gorillas

Nevertheless, some of us who were close to him were worried. Physically, he was far from well. All his life Ake had driven himself unmercifully, with no thought for his health. I do not believe he had ever taken a day of vacation to loaf and really relax, mentally as well as bodily. His variety of interests, I suppose, did give him a change, but that was all. He could, however, relax over a cocktail or a Scotch and soda when he was with people he liked.

In spite of our misgivings, Akeley went to the Lake Kivu district of the Belgian Congo in 1921 and began hunting gorillas on the slopes of Mount Mikeno. A great thrill came when he discovered the marks of four great knuckles in a mud hole, where a gorilla had placed his hand on the ground.

Two days later he saw his first gorillas, after a grueling climb up an almost perpendicular slope, through a jungle so thick that the natives had to cut their way. One of the boys heard a sound across the ravine and pointed to a movement in the bushes. The gorillas were there.

It was too far to shoot, so Akeley and the boys crossed the chasm, climbed the other wall and made their way along the side, just under the crest of the ridge. Suddenly, a deep roar sounded in front of and above them. They went on cautiously for 150 yards when the gunbearer stopped, looking up into the dense tangle directly over their heads. Akeley was in a precarious position on the very edge of the chasm, with only an overhanging four-inch tree between him and the rocks below. The roar sounded again; then came a violent rush. Ake could see nothing at first except the swaying vegetation, but slowly he made out a darker mass — the gorilla's head. The fourth roar was drowned in the thunder of the .475 rifle. Carl said he had only a confused remembrance of what happened next. A great silver-gray body hurtled down upon him, seeming only inches away, and finally stopped against a small tree overhanging the brink of the canyon, its head on one side, feet on the other. That lone tree saved Ake's first gorilla. Had it not caught the 400-pound body, the ape would have crashed into the abyss, from which it could not have been recovered.

Akeley had a tough time skinning the gorilla and getting out the skeleton. All the next day he spent in camp caring for the hide, preserving parts of the soft anatomy and making plaster casts of the hands, feet and face. He was suffering from blood poisoning and should have rested, for hunting the apes on that mountain slope cut with ravines and chasms was like climbing the side of a church steeple. Nevertheless, he went out again as soon as the specimen was safe, and had another exciting experience.

They had worked up and down several ridges, cutting their way through a tangle of vegetation plentifully infused with stinging nettles, when they came upon the trail of a band of gorillas. It led along the side of a steep slope and, had it not been that the great apes travel slowly, feeding as they go, the hunters would never have caught up with them. They followed for about an hour and suddenly heard a rock thunder down into the chasm. The beasts were soon located by the movement of bushes and, from 150 yards, Akeley tried a quick shot with his big gun at a silver-backed male, but missed. Still, the gorillas did not dash away. As a matter of fact, they can't. Their legs are short and weak compared to their heavy torsos, and normally there is no reason for rapid traveling, since they feed on vegetation and do not have to escape enemies. No beast of the jungle wishes to tangle with a gorilla; even a lion would have a poor chance to live, if it came within reach of those mighty arms.

When the men finally caught up with the band, they were again on a steep hillside, with a 200-foot drop into a canyon below them. Ake got himself wedged into a bush, where the kick of the heavy rifle wouldn't dislodge him, and stood ready to shoot. An old black female showed herself directly above him. At the crash of the gun, she fell straight at him. He tried to dodge, but couldn't, and threw himself flat on his face. The dead ape passed right over him, but the mass of green stuff carried with her softened the impact of her great body and he suffered only a bruise on his head. Before Akeley could get up, an avalanche of gorillas followed; huge balls of screaming black fur brushed him as they rolled past. By the time he had recovered and reloaded his rifle, two other gorillas that had been close by had disappeared.

Ake did not think it was a premeditated charge like that of a lion or an elephant, because the female was dead when she fell down the slope. In his opinion, the others had simply followed her, involuntarily, in a blind rush, not knowing she was dead; otherwise, they could very easily have knocked him into the canyon.

The behavior of the gorillas convinced him of the falsity of the idea that they will attack on sight. A half hour later, the men came upon one of the herd which had become lost. It was a 4-year-old male. One of the guides speared the youngster, and Ake says there was a heartbreaking expression of piteous pleading on its face. He thought the baby would have come to his arms for comfort.

The natives insisted that it was impossible to get down to the dead gorilla. They stood listlessly about, shivering in a cold rain, and refused even to attempt the dangerous descent. Akeley, however, would not give up. A man of lesser ideals and courage would not have risked his life for a dead animal, but Ake could not bear the thought of having killed the magnificent beast only to let it rot in the depths of a gloomy canyon. Swinging over the brink on an old tree root, he angled along the face of the cliff, clinging to the vegetation, and eventually reached the stream bed and scrambled up to where the animal lay on a narrow ledge. The natives followed his lead.

Movies of Gorillas

To skin and skeletonize the big ape was a terrific and hazardous business. Only two men could work on the shelf at a time, and they were in imminent danger of crashing into the ravine below. When the job was done, the problem of how to get out confronted them. Ake said the natives were wonderful. Like human flies, they worked their way up the face of an almost perpendicular wall with the heavy loads. At times, he thought none of them would ever reach camp. It was, he admits, the toughest day of his life. He wouldn't do it again for all the museums and gorillas in the world! That's what he said! Personally, I don't believe it.

Anyway, three fine specimens lay under his tent fly — the old male, female and the baby that had been speared. He had death masks of each, skeletons of the adults, and the entire body of the baby preserved in formalin and salt. That would be a priceless anatomical record for sculpture and taxidermy.

But Akeley was a sick man, and the natives wanted to quit, for the going was too tough even for them. With promises of gifts and additional money, he persuaded them to stay. He had one more job to do before he could consider this part of the work successful — motion pictures of gorillas! He told the guides, however, that they must not take him into that hellish place of cliffs and chasms again. No movie camera could operate there and, besides, he was too ill to battle that sort of terrain. The boys promised an easier region, and led him to a saddle between Mounts Mikeno and Karisimbi. Still, it was pretty tough going, and Akeley was just about exhausted when they found a herd of gorillas. Only fifty yards away, he saw a black ball move out on the horizontal branch of a tree. Crouching behind a bush, he set up the movie camera. Meanwhile, a larger gorilla climbed on the same limb. It was a mother with a 2-year-old baby. Almost before he knew it, he was making the first motion picture of gorillas ever taken.

I have seen the film many times. It shows a beautiful background of lush vegetation, with the mother and baby in full view. After a moment, another baby scrambles up a nearby tree. All three of them look at Akeley curiously, but unafraid. The mother pretends indifference and boredom and lies down on one arm as though about to go to sleep. One of the babies seems highly amused. He stands up, slaps his arms against his breast and appears to be roaring with laughter. Then come some close-ups taken with the 6-inch lens. The film gives the impression of a happy family. The great apes act just as a human mother with her two children might act. Certainly, there is no indication that the gorilla is a ferocious animal who would charge a man at sight and tear him apart with pleasure.

A little later, the men discovered another band of ten or twelve gorillas. Akeley watched them across a ravine with his field glasses for some time, as they were too far away for pictures. An old female was lying on her back, yawning and stretching, enjoying a sun bath. He shot one more specimen and then returned to camp. Except for another old male, his group for African Hall was complete.

The Old Man of Karisimbi

Akeley had brought with him two friends from Chicago, Mr. and Mrs. Herbert Bradley, and his secretary, Miss Martha Miller. He wanted one of them to kill the remaining gorilla and sent a message to their camp, two days' march away. Ake was in bad shape physically. He had lost twenty pounds and his body was wracked with fever. Nevertheless, when the Bradleys arrived, he went with them to a bitterly cold camp at 11,000 feet above sea level, to the saddle between Mikeno and Karisimbi. On the second day's hunt, the guides found a huge old male moving about in plain sight only twenty-five yards away. Instead of charging, as he should have done according to the popular idea, the gorilla tried to run. Bradley killed him with a bullet in the neck. He was a magnificent specimen, weighing 360 pounds. Since he had a deformed pelvis due to a former bullet wound, he must have encountered other white men and known their danger, yet he did not attack. Akeley said that he had the face of an amiable giant who would do no harm except in self-defense.

From the spot where the old male had fallen, Ake and his friends looked around. Mount Mikeno stood sharply outlined against a deep blue sky; cliffs in the foreground were clothed with soft green and brown moss, like oriental drapery. Beyond, "the eye swept over a scene of marvelous opalescent colors in which, dimly seen, rose distant mountain ranges, suggestions of shimmering lakes and mysterious forests."

Carl decided this was the perfect setting for the group in African Hall. An artist must make the long trip from New York to put the scene on canvas, but it would be well worthwhile. Never did Akeley's soul more keenly respond to the beauty of nature. Had he known, then, that it would be his final resting place, he would have been well content.

Akeley became so impressed by the lack of accurate information concerning the life and habits of gorillas that a new vision formed in his mind as he left Mount Mikeno and trekked down to his base camp at the White Friars' Mission. He had been outraged, as were other real sportsmen, by what Prince William of Sweden had done in that same region only a short time before. The prince had slaughtered eighteen gorillas in the name of sport. If others followed his example, even to a lesser degree, the animals were doomed to extinction. Why should not a gorilla sanctuary be created by the Belgian government, including Mounts Mikeno, Karisimbi and Visoke, which stand in a triangle by themselves, four miles apart? There were, he judged, about a hundred animals in this area and they probably did not leave it. If these gorillas were protected, they would doubtless become accustomed to man and could be studied in their natural surroundings to great scientific advantage.

Akeley eventually found two ardent supporters for his idea in the Honorable Gustavus Whitely, Belgian Consul-General at Baltimore, and His Excellency, Baron de Cartier de Marchienne, then Belgian Ambassador at Washington. The ambassador placed Akeley's suggestion before His Majesty, King Albert, a confirmed conservationist. As a result, a year before his death Akeley had the satisfaction of seeing the Parc National Albert created in the region he had recommended.

As soon as Ake returned to New York, he set about mounting the gorillas. It was a labor of love if there ever was one. For the first time, the great apes would be shown at home as they really are, instead of the terrible creatures of popular imagination. He knew that if he mounted the Old Man of Karisimbi standing erect and bending a gun barrel between his teeth, his face contorted into an expression of fiendish rage, it would please the public which craves thrills and excitement. But African Hall was dedicated to animals as they are, not as they are supposed to be. Ake's group was a quiet family scene in a setting of wondrous beauty; an exact reproduction of the spot where the big male died. The background was to be painted by an artist who would go to Karisimbi to make his studies; every leaf, every tree, and every blade of grass must be a true and exact copy of nature. Carl did not live to see the group completed, but it now stands at one end of the Akeley African

[135   ]

Hall, a faithful reproduction of his own miniature model.

During the next years, Akeley went through periods of blackest depression and climbed to heights of exaltation. African Hall absorbed him all but completely. His social life became even scantier than it had been before; plans for the hall itself and for the groups in it, lectures to raise money for it and efforts to interest wealthy men who might help to back it, occupied virtually every waking hour. And at the same time he and Delia Akeley, after more than twenty years, came to the parting of the ways and were divorced. Ake was always reserved about his personal life. He threw himself even more fully into his work, and for months spent energy at a rate that would have killed an ordinary man in a week.

Plans for African Hall

Ake always intended African Hall to carry the name of his friend Theodore Roosevelt. He wrote: "The thought that my greatest undertaking was to stand as a memorial to Theodore Roosevelt doubled my incentive. I am giving the best there is in me to make Roosevelt African Hall worthy of the name it bears."

The project ran into large figures. The city must build a new addition to the museum which would cost considerably more than a million dollars. Another million was needed to collect material and complete the groups, bronzes and bas-reliefs. Akeley traveled from one end to the other of the United States lecturing, always with African Hall as his text; he wrote magazine articles, on some of which I assisted him, and a book, *In Brightest Africa;* he talked to every man of wealth he knew or could meet.

During those years, I was commuting between China and America. While in New York, I lived with Professor Henry Fairfield Osborn, president of the American Museum. We talked continually of Akeley. No man was more impressed by his genius and ability than was the professor, but, at times, the financial demands of Ake's conception appalled him. Once he said to me, "Akeley will kill himself before the project can come into completion; then it will be lost. To get New York City to build a new addition at this time is next to impossible. If only he would settle for one of the existing halls we might get somewhere. Won't you talk to him and see what you can do?"

"Yes," I replied, "I'll speak to him if you want me to, but it won't do any good. I've known Ake for many years, and he will never compromise. No existing hall would begin to give him what he demands. It must be perfection or nothing."

I did talk to Ake. I merely repeated Professor Osborn's words, for my heart was not in it. I knew excatly how Akeley felt. Of course, he said no. He pointed to the beautifully constructed scale model of the hall which he had made years before. Everything in miniature from the great herd of elephants in the center, to each of the forty groups, complete with painted backgrounds, foliage and animals. "If I die before it is finished, Roy, the whole concept and plan is there. Eventually, they will come to see that anything but a specially constructed hall would ruin it all."

He told me he felt that up to this time he had been only

[137]

studying his profession; now he was prepared to put the fruit of that study in one great, perfect example which could stand as a pattern for other museums.

"I have a group of trained men who can carry on what I have begun," he said. "Clark, Rockwell, Jones, Raddatz, Limekiller, Potter, Butler and others are all my pupils. They can finish it if I don't live."

Then events began to move. In 1924, Carl married again and the next year the clouds broke away and the sun shone through, with African Hall in the center of its brilliance. Mr. George Eastman asked his friend Daniel E. Pomeroy to get in touch with Carl Akeley. Although 71 years old, Mr. Eastman wanted to go to Africa. Mr. Pomeroy, a trustee of the museum, had long been an admirer of Ake's and an enthusiastic backer of African Hall. He and Akeley went to Rochester, New York, to see Eastman. After describing in his vivid way what the hall would be like, Ake asked Eastman for a million dollars "to create the greatest exhibit in the world."

Mr. Eastman couldn't go along with him to that extent, but he did promise $100,000, plus his share of the expedition's expenses. Mr. Pomeroy offered half that amount, and said he believed another friend of his, Colonel Daniel B. Wentz of Philadelphia, would contribute the cost of a group. Colonel Wentz did. At that meeting, plans were formulated for the Akeley-Eastman-Pomeroy Expedition of 1926–1927. Carl could hardly contain his happiness. His dream was coming true.

During the last few weeks before the expedition's start, I saw Akeley frequently. He worked like a man possessed from seven in the morning until late at night, but was never

so happy. We had dinner together at the Century Club
shortly before he sailed. Sitting in the big library in front of
the fire, Carl talked as I had seldom heard him do. He told
me about his early years, of which I had not known much,
of his hopes and aspirations and how African Hall had come
to dominate his whole life. Memory of the warm clasp of his
hand and the look of affection in his eyes when we said good
night is still fresh in my mind. I left on a lecture trip next
day and never saw him again.

The Last Expedition

He and Mrs. Akeley sailed on January 30, 1926, for England, and then went on to Brussels, where Carl was personally thanked by King Albert for inspiring the Parc National Albert Sanctuary, which had been instituted by
royal decree the previous year. Mr. Eastman and Daniel
Pomeroy later joined them in Africa, as did Rockwell and
Raddatz, two taxidermy and accessory men, and the artists
Leigh and Jansson. Martin Johnson was there, too, on an
expedition, making the film of African life called *Simba*
which Ake had helped to arrange and sponsor. Carl had the
great satisfaction of participating with Martin in photographing lion spearing by Lumbwa natives. That is a high
spot in the film. It was when he had missed getting a similar
spectacle that he had determined to build the camera which
they were both using.

But Akeley had great work of his own to do, and he went
at it with furious energy. During eight months, Carl collected the animals and materials for seven groups — a herculean task. The strenuous effort took its inevitable toll, and

he came down with fever. Against his vehement protests, he was taken back to the Kenya Nursing Home in Nairobi. There he remained three weeks, chafing to get away every moment of the day. Before he had fully recovered he insisted on continuing with his project to visit the gorilla country of Kivu, where the background painting for the group was to be made by the artist Leigh, and where flowers, grass, leaves and other accessories would be collected.

The original plan of the expedition had called for all members of it to return to the United States in October. The immense amount of work done — much more than anyone, probably, except Akeley himself had thought would be possible — had already made the trip a great success, and as autumn came on Eastman and Pomeroy prepared to leave on schedule. But Ake refused to go. No matter how much had been done, there was still more to do, and he could not bring himself to leave it. Eastman and Pomeroy left for the States at last, but Ake determinedly stayed on. Perhaps he suspected that he had not much time left.

While he was assembling the equipment for the trip, his old friend Leslie Tarleton said, "Carl, do you think you are strong enough to undertake that expedition to the Congo?" Ake replied, "The expedition will answer that question." Knowing Carl as I did, I think he never believed he would see Nairobi again, and that he wanted to die in "the most beautiful spot in the world."

Mr. Pomeroy writes in the *Natural History* magazine: "The trip was strenuous. On November 1st, there were many hills to climb, and the heat and humidity were almost unbearable. Akeley became faint and ill and too weak to walk.

He was carried on an improvised hammock for about four miles when a thunderstorm broke and it was necessary to make a temporary camp. The next day he felt better and was able to walk into Kutshuru. Akeley was approaching the country which he loved more than any other on earth and he seemed to be torn between the desire to rest and the great urge to reach the goal."

In spite of his condition, he insisted on ascending to the 11,000-foot saddle between Mounts Mikeno and Karasimbi where he had shot the gorillas. He had to be carried part of the way. It became bitterly cold. The small charcoal fire they were able to provide was only a feeble defense against the glacial frost and his heart was affected by the altitude.

A fierce storm of sleet and snow so saturated the air with moisture that Ake found breathing difficult. Three days after reaching the saddle he died peacefully, relinquishing his great task to those who would carry it on to the end.

Akeley was buried on the slope of beautiful Mount Mikeno in a tomb of solid volcanic rock. A covering of cement bears the legend "Carl Akeley, Nov. 17, 1926."

African Hall, the goal of Akeley's life, was brought to completion by his wife and many friends chief among whom was Daniel E. Pomeroy. It was he who had made the original contact with George Eastman. He gave unstintingly of his time and money, and never ceased until the last group had been installed. To those of us who participated in even a small way, it became a consecrated task, a means by which we could show our respect and devotion to a friend, and to the genius of a great American.

In 1929, New York City granted $1,250,000 for the building. Even though Akeley, in his mind, had dedicated it to Theodore Roosevelt, it was opened on May 19, 1936, the anniversary of Carl's birthday, as the Akeley African Hall. Thirteen hundred guests gathered to pay him tribute in the stately room, redolent of the peace and beauty of the country it portrays. The walls are encased in dark green marble, and silvered bas-relief panels depicting native scenes rest above each case opening. A herd of eight magnificent elephants stand like prehistoric monsters in the center of the darkened room, suggesting the gloom and mystery of the densest jungle. Looking into the lighted groups, one sees Africa itself: stark, waterless deserts, game-dotted plains, majestic mountains, lakes, rivers, and fever-laden swamps. The wildlife is there in sunshine and shadow, its animals standing quietly, resting in the shade of an acacia tree or feeding in the half light of a flower-filled forest, undisturbed by the menace of human enemies. Two million persons every year pass through that hall, each of them attesting, unconsciously, to the greatness of the dream for which Carl Akeley gave his life.

Trails of the World

TO view one's life in retrospect, like pages of history, is illuminating. The mistakes and successes and the important turning points emerge with startling clearness, even though, at the time, they may have seemed obscure. This streamlined autobiography begins in a place, and with an event, that became of paramount importance in my career.

On the thirtieth of August, 1922, the Central Asiatic Expedition, under my leadership, was camped in the very center of Outer Mongolia. All through the summer we had pushed deeper and deeper into the Gobi, using motor cars successfully for the first time in exploration. But now winter might shut in any day. Golden plover were drifting down from the Arctic tundras like wind-blown leaves. Lines of geese and ducks etched black tracings on a leaden sky. Sudden flurries of powder snow dusted the desert. These were signs no explorer could ignore. The Well of the Sweet Water, where we were to rendezvous with our camel caravan, was hundreds of miles away, through unexplored country. If we were caught by one of the terrible Mongolian blizzards we might never be able to reach it.

Between us and the well, nothing was marked in the blank space on the Russian "map" except a range of mountains six thousand feet high. How the motors could negotiate them, I didn't know. Perhaps we could find a pass. But there was no other way, and I told the topographers to lay a compass course directly for the well.

For three days we fought eastward mile by mile. The terrain was very bad for the cars — gravel, sand, ravines, ditches, rocks, and washouts. Never a sign of water. The mountains were on our minds, but not even a hill broke the flat horizon. On the second night the topographers had computed our position from star sights. We had already crossed the "mountains"! They did not exist.

I was worried about water. The big cask and all the bags were dry. The last drop had gone into the cars. Everyone was thirsty. Just before sunset of the third day, three Mongol *yurts* (tents) showed on the desert far off to the south. Where there were people there must be water.

Our photographer, J. B. Shackleford, was with me in the leading car a mile in front of the fleet. I said to him, "You wait here and stop the others when they come. I'll go to the *yurts* and ask where we can find water."

He got out and I drove to the Mongol camp. Only a man and his wife were there. They were terribly frightened by my car. They had never dreamed of anything like it. The woman kneeled in a corner of the tent crying, and when she saw me was violently sick. The man tried to run away. I caught him. Cigarettes and kind words eventually calmed their fears. I gave her a steel mirror. In it she looked at her face for the first time. She seemed pleased, though I don't know why she should have been. The Mongol told me of a well not far away.

When I returned to the cars, all the men were gathered about Dr. Walter Granger, the chief paleontologist. In his hand he held a white skull, eight inches long.

"Take a look at this," he said.

I examined it carefully. It was a reptile, and probably

dinosaur, but I had never seen anything like it. Neither had Granger or Professor Berkey, our geologist.

"Where," I asked, "did you get it?"

"Shackleford found it just over there."

He pointed to the north, where the edge of a red cliff showed above the rim of the plain. Shack said he had told the men in the other cars to wait for me, and then had gone off to investigate. He came to the edge of a great badlands depression and climbed down into it a little way to see what it was like. Right in front of him, resting on a pinnacle of weathered sandstone, was the white skull. He picked it off and hurried back to the cars. Shack's discovery was so important that we knew we had to search further. The Mongol had said the well was on the basin floor. We could camp there for the night, fill up with water, and hunt fossils until dark.

Discovery of the Flaming Cliffs

It was a fantastic place, a vast pink bowl cut out of the plain by the knives of wind and frost and rain. Giant "buttes" stood alone, like strange prehistoric monsters carved from sandstone. There seemed to be castles of the Middle Ages. We could imagine spires and towers, gateways, walls, and ramparts. Chasms ran deep into the rock, cut by a maze of ravines and gullies. At the beginning of darkness, a wild, mysterious beauty lay with the purple shadows in every canyon. In the last rays of the setting sun, the rocks seemed to be on fire. We named the place "The Flaming Cliffs."

As soon as camp was made, all of us scattered over the

basin floor, looking for fossils. Bits of white bone were everywhere. Several men saw skeletons partly exposed in the rock. There was not time to take them out, for night was on us. In the morning it was hard to leave such a wonderful place. It would have been even more difficult had we realized that it was one of the most important localities to natural science ever discovered and would become known in every country of the world! But the feel of snow was in the air. We might be trapped if we delayed even a few hours more. A little later the blizzard struck with Arctic fury. Hundreds of sheep and ponies were lost and frozen. By then we had reached our caravan at the Well of the Sweet Water and were safe.

As soon as we arrived at our Peking headquarters, the unknown reptile that Shackleford had found was sent to New York. Within a few weeks a cablegram came from Professor Henry Fairfield Osborn, president of the American Museum of Natural History. He was profoundly excited. "You have discovered the ancestor of the Ceratopsians," it said in effect. "Go back and get more."

The Ceratopsians, a group of great horned dinosaurs, were old friends of Walter Granger's. They lived seventy or eighty million years ago, and their bones suddenly appear in the upper strata of the Age of Reptiles in America. But where they came from, and when, was a scientific mystery. Our little eight-inch skull gave the answer.

The next year we did go back to the Flaming Cliffs. Summer had come in a day with blistering heat. For a year there had been no rain. The cars traveled over a thirsty land where the scanty vegetation lay brown and shriveled. White rims of alkali marked the beds of former ponds; the desert swam in maddening, wavering mirages. The flowing waves of heat gave fantastic shapes to rocks and bushes; gazelles seemed to dance on air and flying birds to run upon the ground. Lakes with reedy shores and wooded islets appeared where we knew there were no lakes, and somber forests offered the coolness of shaded glens. It was a weird unreal world. Mile after mile passed under the wheels. White skulls of camels and the bones of sheep marked the way. The only signs that man had ever lived in this desolate land were the circular mark of a *yurt*, the ashes of a fire, a wooden bowl grimed with hard, dry food, and the skeleton of a woman. She had been left to die alone upon the desert. Vultures had picked her bones clean of flesh.

At a well in the Valley of the Jewels, a strange thing happened. We had with us a little lame Mongol whom we had christened "Hopalong." His family, and all his relatives, had been murdered by a bandit named Kula, not long before we found him. He knew the unmapped country where we were going. The hot, red sun still hung an hour high when we came into the shallow valley. There was a well two miles away, Hopalong said. It was a very old well, and deep, with good water. A few years ago he and his family had camped there for the summer. We pitched our tents ten yards from the well.

Voices in the Desert

Granger had adopted Hopalong as a camp pet, but it was not a unilateral arrangement. Hopalong also adopted Granger. That night he resolutely refused to sleep with the other Mongols. As a matter of course, he spread his sheep-skin at the foot of Walter's bed, outside the tent door. Midnight came and went. Hopalong had not gone to sleep. He was lying on his back looking up at the stars, when strange vibrations drifted to his ears. Voices that weren't voices, neither human nor animal, rising and dying away only to fill the air again. He was frightened. Scrambling into the tent, he shook Granger. Instantly Walter was awake. Hopalong talked excitedly, pointing through the tent door. Sliding out of the sheepskin bag, Granger buckled his revolver belt about his waist and stepped outside. Every stone and pebble lay in sharp silhouette under the white light of a brilliant moon. He could even see the lines in the palm of his hand. A cool wind rippled the American flag above our tent. For five minutes he gazed across the plain, Hopalong's hand on his arm. Then, from far out in the desert, came subdued, indefinable sounds, eerie and un-earthly. Ghost voices, it seemed, murmuring and whisper-ing, swelling in toneless waves to fade and rise again. "It's like the spirits of the dead talking among themselves," Granger thought.

Stepping into the tent, he put his hand on my forehead.

"Roy, wake up. Something is happening out on the desert."

"What is it?"

"I don't know. Sounds like voices."

In a moment I was outside the tent. For a time we stood in a flat silence. Then the soft, weird undertone began again, quavering into a crescendo without timbre or sub-stance, to die in a shuddering moan like the sob of a lost soul.

[150   ]

I gasped. "For God's sake, what was it? It wasn't real but —I surely heard something!"

Hopalong's face was a gray mask in the moonlight.

"My family's spirits come back to the place where they lived," he whispered.

Suddenly I grabbed Granger's shoulder. "Look, look there. Do you see it? That Thing hovering in the air?"

A shape, filmy as gossamer, formed in the black mouth of the well and floated upward in a long spiral. Two almost transparent arms detached themselves, stretched into slim, wavering fingers, and drifted off into the night. Then other shapes took form like a long line of dancing children, holding hands. The breeze seemed to waft them back and forth till they soared upward and disappeared in the eye of the moon.

I saw them; so did Granger and Hopalong. They were not the figment of just one man's imagination. Three people couldn't see the same thing if it wasn't there! Suddenly, the scream of a great horned owl crashed through the stillness. When it died away, there seemed to be a jagged rent in the night where the sound had been. In a single leap Hopalong was inside the tent, cowering at the far end, a coat over his head. Walter and I stared at the place where the Things had hung in the air, but we saw only the black mouth of the well and shining gravel. The wind died as quickly as it was born, and a cloud drifted over the face of the moon.

For an hour Walter and I smoked our pipes in the tent door, but neither the voices nor the shapes came again. Silence, broken only by the distant howl of a lone wolf, lay thick over the desert.

[151   ]

"Marco Polo described this same thing in his *Travels* when he crossed the Gobi to the court of Kublai Khan," I said. "His story was that the 'voices' enticed travelers out into the desert, where they died of thirst. Sven Hedin heard it and says the Mongols are terrified of the sounds. Some of the Russian explorers tell of them, too. Of course there must be a scientific explanation. I don't believe in ghosts."

Walter grinned. "I don't either, but what we heard, and saw, was real enough."

At breakfast Granger and I spoke of what had happened during the night. Our geologist nodded.

"There is nothing supernatural about it. Yesterday, the sun temperature was one hundred and forty-eight degrees. When I went to bed, the thermometer outside my tent registered seventy-six degrees. That's a drop of seventy-two degrees in only a few hours. It must have been considerably lower by midnight. As I walked over the plain, I noticed that many of the rocks had the sharp edges of recent breaks, and others were cracked. Undoubtedly, the day's terrific heat and the night's sudden cold caused great expansion and contraction. I'm sure that what you heard, and what Marco Polo and Hedin reported, were the sounds made by the fracturing of countless rocks and stones as the cold wind played over the superheated desert. You didn't hear them after the wind ceased.

"Your shapes were a natural phenomenon, like the sounds. When we arrived, I took the temperature of the well-water as usual. It was forty-one degrees. Your ghost, and the dancing girls, were nothing but condensation from the cold well-shaft. Probably the moonbeams got in your eyes and ears, too," he added with a grin.

[152   ]

Thus, it was all satisfactorily explained in the precise light of science. But Hopalong will always believe they were the spirits of his murdered family. About that, I wouldn't know!

Mapping a Mirage

The topographers left next morning an hour before the others. They were making a route map of the unexplored country, and it was slow work. Ten miles beyond our camp, I saw their car stopped on the summit of a little hill, and the chief bending over his plane table. To the west lay a small lake. It looked to be about a mile away.

"Thought I'd better sketch the outline before we go down to it," he said.

Gulls and terns were flying over the mirrorlike surface, and an island of tuli grass stretched a long finger toward the center. I studied it through my field glasses. Slowly I began to realize that something was wrong with the lake; the beach grew indistinct and the tuli island danced about in a most peculiar way.

"You had better wait a little before you do any more on your sketch. I think I'll run over there," I said, starting the engine of my car. In five minutes I was on the "shore" of the "lake" — but there wasn't any shore and there wasn't any lake! Not even a suggestion of water or grass, and the terns were sand grouse. The heads of antelope, wading neck deep in heat waves, made perfect gulls.

Back on the hilltop, I said to the topographer, "You can label your sketch 'Mirage Lake,' for that is what it is. I don't wonder you were fooled. That is the most perfect mirage

I've ever seen. If I hadn't looked through my binoculars, I'd never have guessed it wasn't real."

When the fleet arrived, it was difficult to convince the others that they were not looking at water. We discovered, later, that the mirage was a duplication of Chagan Nor, the White Lake, more than a hundred miles away.

As we traveled westward, the dim outlines of isolated mountain peaks appeared to the south, but gradually formed into a continuous chain. They were the eastern extension of the great Altai range that cuts Mongolia in half. The terrain was difficult. Sand patches, acres of "nigger heads" — hummocks covered with low, thorny bushes — and soft red loam where the cars sank to their hubs. But, just when we were completely exhausted from pushing and hard work, a gravel plain, level as a tennis court, would stretch away for miles to the western horizon. Now and then an ancient camel trail etched a faint tracing across the desert. We followed it if possible, because there would be wells, but usually drove on a compass course, mapping the country on both sides. The Russian map was almost useless. It had been compiled years ago, largely from native information and few actual surveys. Even the main control points were incorrectly located by latitude and longitude.

Dinosaur Eggs

It was a great day for the Central Asiatic Expedition when we pitched our tents for the second time at the Flaming Cliffs. Almost immediately the men went down into the basin. By evening each of us had discovered a dinosaur skeleton. The place seemed to be paved with fossil bones.

On the second day, at noon, George Olsen, one of the paleontologists, came into camp with a strange story. He said he had discovered some petrified eggs. All of us joked him about it at first. We thought they would prove to be stones shaped like eggs.

"Laugh if you want to," George said, "but they are eggs, all right. Come with me."

We had to walk only a short distance from camp. Olsen pointed to a small rock ledge. There lay three objects shaped like eggs. They were about eight inches long. Dr. Granger picked one up and all of us gathered around him. The egg was heavy, for the inside was solid red sandstone. The pebbled shell looked exactly like regular eggshell, only thicker. It was brown and completely mineralized. Granger shook his head.

"I'm darned if I can figure it out. This is a Cretaceous deposit, but there were no Cretaceous birds big enough to lay an egg this size. Anyway, it isn't shaped like a bird's egg. And there are nothing but dinosaur bones here. I wonder if this could be a dinosaur egg? We don't know how dinosaurs reproduce. Most reptiles lay eggs, and dinosaurs were reptiles. Probably they did lay eggs. But none have been found anywhere in the world. Believe it or not, I think we are looking at the first dinosaur egg ever seen by human eyes."

The three eggs evidently had broken out of the sandstone ledge beside which they lay. Other shell fragments were partially embedded in the rock, and just under the shelf we could see the ends of two more eggs. While the rest of us were on our hands and knees about the spot, George Olsen began to scrape away the loose rock on the summit of the ledge. To our amazement, he uncovered the skeleton of a small dinosaur, lying four inches above the eggs! This was a type completely new to science. It was only four feet long, and toothless, although full grown. Professor Osborn named it *Oviraptor* (the egg seizer) and he believed that it lived by feeding upon the eggs of other dinosaurs. Possibly it was in the very act of digging up this nest when it was overcome by a sandstorm and buried upon the eggs it had come to steal.

In shape the eggs are elongated, much like a loaf of French bread. Two of them, broken in half, show the white bones of little unhatched dinosaurs. The preservation is beautiful. Some of the eggs have been crushed, but the pebbled surface of the shells is as perfect as though they had been laid yesterday instead of seventy or eighty million years ago. Fine sand had filtered through the breaks and the interior of all the eggs is hard sandstone. A later microscopical examination showed that the air canals in the shells are quite different in shape and arrangement from those of birds, turtles, or reptiles, and proved that the white bones showing in the core of several of the specimens, really are the skeletons of unhatched baby dinosaurs.

A few days after the first discovery, five eggs were found in a cluster. Albert Johnson also obtained a group of nine. Each member of the expedition became an enthusiastic egg hunter and everyone had success. Altogether, twenty-five eggs were removed. Some of them were lying on the surface, exposed by erosion; others were enclosed in rock with only the ends showing, and one nest in soft, disintegrated sandstone could be excavated with a whisk broom.

The deposit was unbelievably rich. Seventy-five skulls and

skeletons of small dinosaurs were discovered, several of them absolutely perfect. Obviously, the Flaming Cliffs was a region of great concentration for dinosaurs during the breeding season. Like present-day reptiles, dinosaurs scooped out shallow holes and laid their eggs in circles with the ends pointing inward; sometimes there were three tiers of eggs, one on top of the other. The lady dinosaur covered her eggs with a thin layer of sand and left them to be hatched by the sun's rays. She didn't sit on them like a hen. The covering sediment must be loose and porous, in order to admit warmth and air, and it is probable that the exceedingly fine sand at this spot was particularly well adapted to act as an incubator.

During a windstorm, many feet of sand might be heaped over some of the nests. Thus the eggs never hatched. As time went on, more and more sand piled up. Finally, it became so heavy that the shells cracked. When the liquid contents ran out, sand sifted into the shells and formed a core. That kept the eggs in their original shape. After many thousands of years the sand over the eggs was consolidated into rock. Such was the story.

Eggs Capture the World

None of us dreamed at that time what the discovery of these dinosaurs' eggs would mean to the future of the expedition, and particularly to me. Of course we realized they were interesting and important, but new discoveries in other branches of science were crowding in on us so rapidly that the dinosaur eggs merely took their place in the process of revealing a new continent scientifically. It was not until we returned to Peking that I began to understand what a fantastic situation the eggs had created.

At our first news conference, fifteen correspondents of the world's greatest newspapers gathered in the drawing room of our headquarters at Number Two Kung Hsien Hutung. They seized upon the dinosaur-egg story like a cat pouncing on a bird, and rushed to the telegraph office. Within a few hours the news had gone to the ends of the earth. At that time a good-sized civil war was being fought between Peking and Shanghai. The staid London *Times* wired its correspondent: "Restrict war news to thirty words. Give Andrews' expedition unlimited cable coverage."

We all realized, of course, that the eggs had caught the popular fancy, but no one was prepared for what happened later. It was important for me to return to America in order to raise another quarter of a million dollars for the extension of the expedition both in time and scope. I sailed for Seattle via the northern route. At Victoria reporters swarmed aboard the ship. A representative of the Seattle *Post Intelligencer* said, "I will give you fifteen hundred dollars for the exclusive use of the dinosaur eggs photograph for a week." Another reporter offered three thousand, and a San Francisco paper upped it to five thousand dollars. They came like bids at an auction sale. I was aghast. I told them, "I'll give you the news story but I'm not selling the photographs. After we reach New York I'll see how best to give everyone an equal chance."

Enroute across the continent newsmen swarmed aboard the train at almost every stop, and the photographers' flash bulbs blazed. New York was the same, only more so. It was exciting, and great fun, although somewhat bewildering.

Dinosaur eggs! Dinosaur eggs! That was all I heard. At first I was embarrassed, and somewhat indignant. The Central Asiatic Expedition had made many other dramatic discoveries, more important even than the dinosaur eggs, and I wanted them to receive due attention. I didn't wish to be known only as "the big-egg man." But the eggs held the spotlight.

Not even a psychologist can explain that indefinable "something" that makes a play, a song, a book, or a dinosaur egg, catch the public fancy. Probably part of it was because nearly everyone has an egg for breakfast, and sometimes they aren't too fresh. A crotchety husband could torment his wife with a remark like, "I suppose this is one of Andrews's seventy-million-year-old dinosaur eggs. It surely tastes like it." And, of course, dinosaurs, to most people, are semi-mythical creatures born of a bad dream, which lived in the dim, dark days when the earth was young. Anyway, the eggs were the basis of countless popular jokes which appeared in newspapers and magazines and made cocktail conversation. They were, too, a godsend to cartoonists and comic-strip artists. For weeks, one of the great New York papers carried a series every day of what was going on in the dinosaur world. Professor Osborn said they did more in a few weeks to make the man-in-the-street "dinosaur conscious" than all the paleontological research of half a century. Eventually, I became philosophical about it, and realized that it was proving of enormous value to the expedition. I had only to look back ten years and remember my old friend Vilhjalmur Stefanssen's "Blond Eskimos"! That was a similar case.

"Stef" was a young anthropologist and explorer who had

been plugging along without too much recognition. His work in the Arctic was original and very valuable, but about the least sensational of any explorer I have ever known because he always played down his extraordinary experiences.

He found a new tribe of Eskimos in the unknown Coppermine River Region. Some of them were blessed with blue eyes and light hair, instead of the traditional brown eyes and raven locks, and he remarked that this might *possibly* be the result of too close familiarity with the unknown survivors of the lost Sir John Franklin expedition, which had perished in the vicinity in 1848. That was one of the tragedies of the Arctic. After abandoning their ice-trapped ships, the *Erebus* and *Terror*, 129 men tried to make their way overland to civilization. The mystery surrounding their ultimate fate, and the suggestion that some of them might have lived for years with the Coppermine Eskimos, leaving their "footprints on the sands of time," was too good a story for any live reporter to miss. The blond Eskimos became the topic of the day, and carried Stefanssen to fame on the strength of their newspaper value. Not that his geographical discoveries, and fine scientific work, were of any less importance, but he might have plugged away for years without the public recognition he deserved, had not this particular story caught the popular fancy.

"Stef" was outraged, at first, just as I was when my turn came. We both wanted the serious results of our work to be the measure of its publicity. Nevertheless, it was due to the blond Eskimos that the Canadian Government offered to finance his next expedition in a big way. What the blond Eskimos did for Stefanssen, the dinosaur eggs did for me. On the platter with the eggs, the newspaper served up a lot of solid information as to what the expedition had accomplished in other fields. The copious printer's ink enabled me to raise the second quarter of a million dollars much more quickly than would have been possible otherwise.

"*How Did You Start Exploring?*"

During that frenzied period, and often later, people asked me, "How did you start exploring and digging up dinosaur eggs in the Gobi Desert?"

The answer is simple: "I couldn't help it. I was born that way."

I first saw the light of day on January 26, 1884, and from the time that I can remember anything, I always intended to be a naturalist and explorer. There never was any choice. It was written in the Book. The Hand that writes in the Book is one over which we have no control. Very early my parents recognized that fact. Instead of trying to direct my interests along stereotyped lines, they let me range the woods and fields of our southern Wisconsin home, at Beloit, to my heart's content. My boyhood, in some respects, was curiously like those of Admiral Robert E. Peary and Carl Akeley. All of us loved nature so passionately that we could only be happy out of doors. Like them, I taught myself taxidermy and paid most of my expenses in Beloit College by mounting birds and animals.

My ambition was to join the staff of the American Museum of Natural History in New York. To work in such a museum, and to go out on expeditions, would be pure heaven. Just before I graduated from college in 1906, I

[161]

wrote to Dr. Bumpus, the director. He replied that no position in the museum was open, that if I were in New York at any time he would be glad to see me — but, of course, not to come unless I had other business in the city. That was quite enough for me. A week after graduation I was on my way to New York with thirty dollars in my pocket and two days' luncheon in a shoebox.

At eleven o'clock on July 6, 1906, I confronted the majestic façade of the American Museum of Natural History. Feeling very small, I was admitted to the director's office in the east tower room on the fifth floor. Years later, when I, myself, sat in that same director's chair, and young men and women came to see me, obviously frightened half to death, I remembered with a tug at my heart how I felt that day. But Dr. Bumpus couldn't have been more friendly. He was tall and spare, with thinning hair and a small black mustache. An air of great vitality and tremendous energy being held in check dominated his personality. He seemed like a racehorse at the post ready to leap down the track at the starter's signal.

We talked for some time, or rather I did, for he only sat there asking me questions. At last he said, regretfully, that there wasn't a position of any kind open in the museum. My heart dropped into my shoes. Finally I blurted out:

"I'm not asking for a position. I just want to *work* here. You have to have someone to clean the floors. Couldn't I do that?"

"But," said he, "a man with a college education doesn't want to clean floors."

"No," I said, "not just *any* floors. But the museum floors

are different. I'll clean them and love it if you'll let me." His face lighted with a smile.

"If that's the way you feel about it, I'll give you a chance. You will get forty dollars a month. You can start in the Department of Taxidermy with James L. Clark. Now come to lunch with me. Then I'll introduce you to Clark and the others." I remember what we had for lunch — cold salmon and green peas at a restaurant called the Rochelle on Columbus Avenue.

First Months in the Museum

My duties in the museum consisted of first mopping the floor in the morning, straightening up the room, mixing clay, and doing all the odd jobs of an assistant to Jimmy Clark, whom I liked better the longer I knew him. There was no place in New York so fascinating to me as the museum, and I have never been happier than in those early months. Jim had a horror of wasting a moment of time, and so did I. Every Sunday, every holiday, and usually far into the night, both of us could be found busy on our separate interests somewhere in the building.

Director Bumpus did not forget me down there in the taxidermy department. He would send for me frequently to write special labels or do some other bit of work for him. He used to inspect my floor now and then to see if the college diploma had got in the way of the mop. After eight weeks I was given a five-dollar-a-month raise. That enabled me to eat a little better.

I had been in the museum only a few months when my

big chance came. In the director's office I was introduced to a fussy little gray-haired gentleman named Richardson. He was, Dr. Bumpus said, going to build a life-sized model of a whale out of paper, to hang in the third-floor gallery well. I was to be his assistant. I was considerably frightened but tried not to show it. What I knew about whales was less than nothing. I had never met a whale in Wisconsin's Rock River! But the job wasn't as terrifying as it sounded, for we were only to enlarge a scale model which Jim Clark had made under the direction of Dr. F. A. Lucas, director of the Brooklyn Museum.

We got along all right at first, because Richardson knew what he was doing until it came to the paper covering. The framework of angle iron and basswood strips was impressive, for the whale boasted a length of seventy-six feet. But the paper wouldn't work. It buckled and cracked and sank in between the ribs. Our whale looked perfectly awful. It seemed to be in the last stages of starvation. I used to dream about it at night and the director was in despair.

Finally he called Jimmy Clark and me to his office. "This whale is getting on my nerves," he said. "It is beyond all endurance. What shall we do?"

Jimmy and I knew exactly what to do, for we had spent many hours discussing that emaciated whale. "Fire the paper gentleman," we said, "and let us finish it with wire netting and papier-mâché."

The director beamed. "Done. If you turn that wreck of a cetacean into a fat, respectable whale, I'll give you both a knighthood."

Jimmy and I hopped to it with a crew of twelve men. It was amazing what a well-regulated diet of papier-mâché did

[164   ]

for that whale. He lost the pitiful, starved appearance, his sides filled out and became as smooth as a rubber boot. We could almost feel him roll and blow as we built him up with our new tonic. After eight months the job was done. During forty-seven years our whale has hung in the gallery, and is still as good as new. He has been stared at by millions of eyes, for he is still one of the most popular exhibits in the museum.

The Amagansett Whale

Building that whale marked an important turning point in my life. It graduated me from floor scrubbing, taught me something about handling men, and set me thinking and reading about whales. Then Fate dealt me another ace. A real honest-to-goodness whale was killed off the Long Island coast, at Amagansett. Jim Clark and I were sent to get the skeleton. The director's instructions, as we dashed into and out of his office, were: "Get the whole thing. Photographs, measurements, baleen, and skeleton — every bone."

Once we had arrived at the village, the business of buying the whale was quickly done. The baleen, or whalebone, was the valuable part, for at that time it was still being used for corsets and carriage whips. I believe it cost us thirty-two hundred dollars, which was only a little more than the commercial value. They threw in the skeleton, but we were obligated to get the bones ourselves.

The carcass was beached just at the edge of low tide. After the fishermen had stripped off the blubber, they went away. Jimmy and I were faced with a real problem, for the skeleton lay embedded in some fifty tons of flesh. Of course we could do nothing alone, and the fishermen were not at all keen to work, even for high wages. The thermometer stood at twenty above zero and the wind was bitter. Finally we did persuade half a dozen men to hack away at the carcass with great knives. A horse helped to drag off chunks of meat by means of ropes and hooks. Then the worst happened. A storm blew up from the east, beating upon the exposed coast with near-hurricane force. We saw it coming, and anchored our whale as best we could, working hip-deep in the icy water.

For three days the shore was a smother of white surf. Anxiously we waited. Only half the skeleton was on the beach, and that would be well-nigh worthless if the remainder were lost. The fourth day was dead calm, but very cold: twelve degrees above zero at noon. When we got to the beach, a smooth expanse of sand, innocent of whale, met our eyes. The bones had disappeared! Jim and I were frantic, but the anchor ropes extended down into the sand where the bones had been. A little shoveling exposed the skeleton, deeply buried. It would have been difficult enough, in the best circumstances, to uncouple the huge vertebrae, and get the ribs of the lower side, but now it was almost impossible. As soon as we dug out a shovelful of sand to get at a bone, the depression filled with water. We had to grope blindly with small knives, our arms in the freezing water up to the shoulders, to disarticulate each vertebra. Jim and I carried on alone for three days, warming our hands every few minutes over a driftwood fire. The villagers wouldn't work even for high wages. It was too cold. It seemed hopeless, but the director had told us get every bone, and we simply couldn't give up. At last some of the fishermen decided to help, and at the end of the week the skeleton lay well up on the beach. We returned to New York with a clean bill of bones.

I was allowed to describe the Amagansett whale, and wrote my first scientific paper. Moreover, study of whale literature made it clear that there was very little accurate knowledge about the habits and life histories of the animals. No enthusiastic young naturalist ever had a more virgin field for study.

My First Live Whale

Three shore whaling stations had recently been established on the west coast of Vancouver Island and southeastern Alaska. The great beasts were hunted from little ninety-foot steamers, killed with an explosive harpoon shot from a small cannon, towed to the factories on shore, and converted into oil and fertilizer. It was a priceless opportunity for study and the collecting of specimens. When I told the director I would go without salary if he would pay my expenses, he was pleased. Thus, in the spring of 1908 I set out on my first real expedition.

Twenty miles up the great gash which Barclay Sound cuts into the west side of Vancouver Island, the whaling factory huddled against a fir-clad mountain. I came to it in a little coastal steamer, weak from seasickness, which plagued me all my whaling years. Nevertheless, I went out on the hunting vessels almost daily. With nothing to distract my mind except a heaving stomach, I could time how long whales remained at the surface when feeding, how often they blew, how they used their flippers and flukes, and a hundred other details which no whale killer had time to note in the heat of battle.

Never will I forget the first time a whale came up beside the ship. I saw the animal rising when it was still far below the surface. A huge, ghostly shape driving swiftly upward until it erupted like a submarine volcano beside the vessel. I could look down into the cavernous nostrils as they swelled out and shot a geyser of vapor almost into my face. A second later the explosion of the harpoon gun sent me reeling backward. Crawling to the rail, I had a momentary glimpse of a great tail rising and falling in a smashing blow that could have crushed our little boat to splinters. Then dead quiet except for the slow rattle of the rope as the lifeless body sank straight down into the blue depths. Once again it happened before I could steel my nerves to think and act. Then, with my face pressed into the camera hood, I waited to press the button until the phantom body showed in the mirror.

There was always the fascination of wondering what went on beneath the surface when we hunted a school of whales. Often I saw them feeding quietly, perhaps a mile apart, and then, at some signal, they would heave their vast bulks into the air and disappear at the same instant. They might double and reappear behind the ship, breaking water in line like a company of soldiers marching on parade. At that time I could not guess how they communicated with each other, but recently sonic apparatus has detected an amazing variety of sounds made by the animals. But how can they descend to depths where the water pressure is tremendous and return to the surface a few minutes later with the rush of a leaping salmon? Too-rapid emergence is the terror of the deep-water diver, because his body is then twisted and racked by the deadly "bends," but it doesn't seem to bother a whale.

It was positively indecent the way I pried into the private lives of whales during those days at sea. With field glasses I watched from the masthead, the love-making of a pair of humpback whales fifty feet long. It was the first time the mating act had ever been described by a scientist. An amorous bull whale may be very amusing to us, but to his lady friend he is doubtless as exciting as a matinee idol is to a debutante. In this particular case, the gentleman whale executed a series of acrobatic performances, evidently with the object of impressing the female and arousing her libido. First, he stood on his head with the tail and fifteen feet of body out of the water. The great flukes waved slowly at first; then faster and faster until the water was pounded into foam and the terrific slaps on the surface could be heard a mile away. Then he slid up close to the female, rolling over and stroking her with his right flipper, which weighed almost a ton. She lay on her side, apparently enjoying his caresses. Then he backed off and dived. I thought he had left her for good, but she lay quietly at the surface. She knew full well that he would not desert her— yet! He was gone for, perhaps, four minutes; then with a terrific rush he burst from the water, throwing his entire fifty-foot body diagonally into the air. It was a magnificent effort and I was proud of him. Falling back in a cloud of spray, he rolled over and over up to his lady love, and clasped her with both flippers. It was all over in an instant. Both whales lay at the surface, blowing slowly, exhausted by emotion.

I felt embarrassed to be spying on their love-making like a

Peeping Tom, but the captain was made of sterner stuff. The exhibition left him cold. His materialistic mind visualized, to the exclusion of all else, the thousands of dollars their carcasses would bring in oil and fertilizer. From the masthead I pleaded with him a "have a heart," but without avail. The ship slid closer and closer to the half-slumbering lovers, and a bomb-harpoon crashed into the side of the amorous bull. Half an hour later the lady, too, was killed, for she refused to leave the vicinity of her dead lord.

Birth of a Baby Whale

I may still be the only naturalist who has ever been present at the birth of a baby whale. One day a big female finback was brought to the station, obviously in an "interesting condition." The captain told me he had killed her only a few miles from shore, where she was probably seeking quiet water for the accouchement. Wire cables were made fast about her flukes, and, as the steam winch drew the sixty-ton body out of the water, the baby was born right before our eyes. It was twenty-two feet long and would weigh about fifteen tons; the mother measured sixty-five feet. Of course the reason why the babies are so proportionately large is that whales live in a supporting medium.

Milk was oozing from the teats of the whale, and I drew off a pail full just like milking a cow. The taste was not good but it was so strongly impregnated with the gases of decomposition that I imagine not much of the original flavor was left.

Absolutely nothing was known about the breeding habits of cetaceans, so I went into the study in a big way. The uterus of an eighty-foot sulphur-bottom whale is about as big as a double bed, and hunting for an embryo is a messy job. Nevertheless, I obtained about two dozen. By recording the size of each fetus and the dates it became evident that there is no regular breeding season for whales, although the "joys of spring" seem to have a slight effect upon their love-making. We can never know whether or not whales have any constancy in their marital relations. But with the whole ocean to roam in, I should judge that free love was the order of their lives. Still, their great hearts, as big as an office safe, do know the tender feelings of affection — at least mother love — as I have seen many times.

By the end of the summer, I had obtained the skeleton of a humpback whale for the museum and my notebooks contained more new data about dead and living whales than had ever been gathered before. The reason, of course, was that I happened to be the first naturalist to study whales at sea with the unequaled opportunities which the shore stations presented.

The photographs of living whales created a mild sensation in the newspapers, for mine were the only pictures ever taken, up to that time, of the biggest and least-known group of mammals in the world. I wrote my first article for a popular magazine, the *World's Work*, began to give public lectures on whales, and entered Columbia University to study for the degree of Doctor of Philosophy. In the meantime, I had been transferred to the Department of Mammals and Birds, under the great naturalists, Drs. J. A. Allen and Frank M. Chapman. Instead of receiving an increase in salary, the director allowed me to work at the museum in the mornings, and at the university in the afternoons. I was getting a hundred dollars a month, and that was quite enough, for I did not have time for any social life outside my work. Part of my study was comparative anatomy, at the College of Physicians and Surgeons, then at 59th Street, off Columbus Avenue. The old building itself was informal, and our student life followed its pattern. I used to work there far into the night as well as all Sundays and holidays. Two o'clock in the morning often found me bent over a dissecting table under a single drop light, surrounded by corpses in various stages of disrepair.

I did a good deal of lecturing that winter. I enrolled with the Department of Education of New York City, and, at ten dollars a night, learned lecturing the hard way. At some of the dates they wouldn't start until the police had arrived. If the audience didn't like the lecturer they might plaster him with tomatoes or overripe eggs. But it was a real challenge. If you could interest these people you were good. Later I came to the J. B. Pond Bureau, which had sponsored Admiral Peary, Amundsen, Sir Ernest Shackleton, Carl Akeley, and other famous explorers. In later years, I used to say that very few people in the United States had escaped hearing me lecture. But lecturing is as essential to an explorer as is writing. If you are depending upon the public for financial support, you must tell them what you have done and what you are planning to do.

In the spring of 1909, I made a short expedition to the St. Lawrence and Saguenay Rivers for white porpoises; my companions were French-Canadians who did not speak a word of English. We hoped to bring a porpoise back alive for the New York Aquarium, but conditions were not right and they could not be netted. Nevertheless, I did shoot and harpoon four fine specimens, and made a plaster cast of the largest. It hangs now in the Hall of Ocean Life at the American Museum.

Only a month after returning from the St. Lawrence, I was off again, this time to wander in the far places of the world. One day the director called me to his office. "Would you like to go to Borneo and the Dutch East Indies?" he asked. Just like that! Would I like to go to Paradise?

Off to the East Indies

"The U. S. Bureau of Fisheries have asked if I will lend you to them for a cruise on the *Albatross*. They want to explore some of the small islands of the East Indies, and do deep-sea dredging. Your job will be to study the porpoises and to collect land mammals and birds wherever possible. You are to join the *Albatross* in the Philippines. The northern route across the Pacific will be the quickest."

It was all very matter of fact to him, but I went out walking in a dream. In the first place, the *Albatross* was the most famous ship of her kind afloat. No other exploring vessel was so well equipped for deep-sea dredging, and her personnel had included some of America's most distinguished naturalists. To be numbered in that group was sufficient in itself, even without the prospect of voyaging among the enchanted islands of the East Indies.

Within a month, I was in Manila. The *Albatross*, I learned, was in the south, near Zamboanga, and would not return for several weeks. I wanted to get busy at once, and called upon Dean C. Worcester, Secretary of the Interior for the

Philippines. He was a well-known ornithologist, and during early bird-collecting expeditions had traveled over most of the Philippines. He told me of a small island off the track of ordinary vessels which he had long wanted to explore. I could go there on one of the government's coastal boats.

A week later, on a glorious tropical morning, I was rowed with two Filipino boys toward the low shores of a palm-clothed island. Emerald-green water covered the outlying coral reef over which floated fish painted in rainbow colors. We landed on a sandy beach in a little bay, and made a rapid reconnaissance of the island. It was uninhabited but had a spring of good water; that was the important thing. After leaving food for five days and our collecting gear, the ship steamed away.

I was Robinson Crusoe with two "men Fridays." We made camp beside a huge rock and swung ships hammocks from the branches of an overhanging tree to be well away from the land crabs. Disgusting creatures, these crabs, which swarm over a dead or wounded animal, literally eating it alive. Half the specimens caught in my traps during the night were devoured before I could rescue them in the early morning. There was one family of monkeys on the island, and a few smaller mammals, but the place was alive with birds. Parrots flashed among the trees, and beautiful cream-white pigeons with black wings and tails filled the air with soft cooings and fluttering wings.

Each morning I was up at the first flush of dawn to run the traps, explore every nook and cranny of the island, and shoot new birds. Then back to camp for a swim off the beach before settling down with the boys to skinning and preparing the day's specimens. In the afternoons we waded the tide pools, collecting fish, crabs, snails, and everything that moved and was alive. The glorious weather held without a break. Hot during the day, of course, but we wore nothing but a pair of trunks, and the nights were always cool.

For five days I lived in a glow of ecstatic happiness and bemoaned the fact that the ship would return to end my island dream. But on the fifth day the sun set, and the velvet darkness shut down like a curtain, with no vessel showing on the horizon. The next day came and went, and the next. Still no ship. Our food was gone — even to the last ship's biscuit — but I still had a few shotgun shells and these gave us pigeons.

The Filipino boys began to worry. I didn't care; I was too happy. When the ammunition was gone, I had the natives weave a net out of palm fibers. This we strung over a favorite roosting tree of the black and white pigeons and the first evening snared more than fifty. Fish were easy enough to catch on the reef, and we evaporated sea water and found salt along the edges of the tide pools. With pigeons, fish, crabs and salt, we certainly could not starve.

For two weeks we lived like real castaways. Then one day a streamer of smoke showed against the sky, and the tiny vessel nosed her way toward the island. With my glasses I could see the captain pacing back and forth on the bridge, but we stayed hidden. A boat dropped over the side and two sailors beached it in our little cove. They found us just dipping into a pot of pigeons stewed with palm shoots, and we gave them a share in halves of coconut shells. Packing up our few belongings at the camp beside the rock wrung my heart, for I knew that never again would I have such utter content

[175]

as had been my lot that fortnight while living as a castaway. The captain I found in a fever of anxiety. When he learned how happy and comfortable we had been, he was utterly disgusted. The ship had damaged its propeller and he had worried frightfully for fear we would starve on our desert island before he could return.

Adventure with a Python

When I joined the *Albatross* at Cavite she steamed southward through the Sulu Sea, with only a momentary stop at Twao, British North Borneo, and then on to Sibattik Island for coal. It was a breathless day of torrid heat when she dropped anchor in Sibattik Bay. I can see in memory the sheer wall of jungle; the giant camphor wood and "king trees" stretching up and up till their summits seemed to touch the sky; the palms and creepers and ropes of vines bristling with thorns like the barbed-wire entanglements of a battle front. I can hear the myriad singing insects which filled the air with such a medley of shrill vibrations that my eardrums ached. Then, at four o'clock in the afternoon, all was still. Utter silence lay over the jungle while great billowing clouds rolled swiftly in from the sea, and torrents of rain poured out of the sky. Abruptly the downpour ceased, to leave the jungle steaming like a caldron. Then the insects began again, shrilling louder than before, and the forest creatures took up their separate lives where they had been interrupted by the flood of rain.

I remember, too, my first attempt at moving through the jungle. I tried to force my way — but only once. Thorns and barbs caught and held me in a dozen places. "Wait-a-bit" vines laced my chest and dug deep into my arms and legs. Every move was agony. There was nothing to do but detach them one by one and cut my way to freedom.

All my life I have loathed snakes; I have to force myself to touch them and yet I have injected and brought back hundreds for the museum. Of course, I supposed there would be dozens of snakes in the jungle, and, dutifully, I did try to find them, but the vegetation was so thick, and many of them are so protectively colored, that they eluded me completely. There was, however, one shining exception. I was following a deer trail with my Filipino boy, Miranda, when suddenly he jerked me violently backward.

"Excuse, Master, but right there, big snake. You shoot him, quick." He pointed and I looked, but to no avail. I couldn't see any snake. A great tree overhung the path and Miranda kept saying, "There, there, don't you see him? Right on that branch."

Suddenly a breath of wind shifted the leaves, and a patch of sunlight filtered down to rest upon a glittering eye, in a great flat head pressed upon the branch. Following it back, I made out yards and yards of snake stretched along the tree trunk, poised to drop upon anything that moved. I backed off and lined my sights upon that shining eye. At the crack of the rifle, a typhoon seemed to have struck the jungle. A writhing, twisting mass of flesh and muscle mowed down bushes, crushed small trees, and wrapped itself in a mass of thorny vines and creepers. Miranda and I ran. At a safe distance we watched until the storm quieted; then cautiously ventured back. The snake lay there, still jerking spasmodically, looped and coiled upon the ground. The head was smashed to a pulp. When we straightened out the body,

I paced the length. It measured twenty feet. The stomach was empty and the great serpent must have been very hungry. It was lying above the game trail ready to throw its coils about anything that passed below. Without doubt Miranda's sharp eyes saved me from a horrible death.

Because the *Albatross* had explored the sea bottom from the Philippines to Borneo, she did no hydrographic work until we crossed the Celebes Sea. In those waters, blue as indigo, she dropped her nets sometimes a mile straight down to the ocean floor. Usually the dredge contained a great mass of ice-cold mud, but as this was washed away strange sea creatures began to appear from out of the muck. Animals from the complete darkness of a submarine world where the water pressure was enormous. There were fish with eyes far out on stalks; others bearing phosphorescent spots along the sides like the glowing portholes of a light ship; fish carrying little lanterns in front of their noses to light the way. Sometimes, in the sudden ascent to the surface and release from the terrific pressure, they were turned almost inside out. Usually those from the greatest depths were badly damaged.

Poisoned Stakes at Buru

On the wild mountain island of Buru, then but partially explored, we met the only unfriendliness from natives. The Dutch governor at Ternate had warned us about Buru, but when we landed there not a single native was visible. I went far inland along the edge of a stream with two sailors. Sev-

eral times we found Malay huts, evidently hurriedly abandoned, for fires were still burning and food half eaten. The
strange feeling that unseen eyes were peering from the jungle made us definitely uncomfortable, but never could we
catch sight of a human being. We had been following a trail
along the stream, and when it was time to return I explored
it cautiously. Sure enough, we found what I feared. Sharp-
ened bamboo stakes, probably poisoned, set at an angle
along the trail, just where they would jab us in the
thighs. It was a Malay trick of which I had often heard.
Abandoning the path, we worked down the stream bed
to the shore. I, for one, was devoutly thankful to see the
boat.

Every day of the cruise was filled with interest and excitement. Often I was dropped off on tiny, uninhabited islands to spend a day or two while the ship dredged in the
vicinity. We hunted sambur deer as big as American elk; the
strange wild boar, babirusa, with tusks growing up through
the snout; monkeys of half a dozen species; and crocodiles.
The birds were bewildering in their numbers and beauty. It
was a paradise for a naturalist.

When the *Albatross* returned to the Philippines she tar-
ried less than a fortnight at Cavite, because her three-year
Oriental cruise was ended. Steaming northward, dredging
on the way, she touched the southern end of Formosa,
where I collected new mammals and birds; then on to the
little village of Soo Wan in the north.

Soo Wan came near to being the last earthly port of call
for the *Albatross* and all her crew, for we ran full into a
young typhoon sweeping up the Formosa Channel. I had always wanted to experience a typhoon; it should be a part

of anyone's Oriental education. One is quite enough, however. It came with amazing suddenness, catching us when we were halfway to Keelung, forty miles from Soo Wan. In the beginning we passed a small, low-lying British gunboat. She was only a few fathoms off our port beam when a man started aft, presumably to hoist her colors. I was watching through my binoculars and saw a great, green sea lap over her stern, sweeping the man off the deck like a straw. It was pretty awful seeing that man disappear so quickly into the smother of white-topped waves. Neither did it help our peace of mind, for we had begun to realize that the gallant old *Albatross* might end her twenty-eight years of service at the bottom of the sea. In a few hours, perhaps, we ourselves would feel the strangling water closing over our heads. A tense calmness pervaded the ship. We were fighting a battle for life against the elements, and the odds were on their side. No one talked much, for it was difficult to hear above the shrieking gale and crashing water.

The *Albatross* was headed directly into the mountainous green waves, which broke over the bow and swept the deck every time her nose went down. A mile away, on the port side, sheer cliffs rose like a wall above a narrow beach smothered in white foam. For some reason the captain had decided to fight his way against the rising storm up the coast instead of riding it out in the open sea. Keelung was only twenty miles to the north, but often we barely held our own. Foot by foot the old ship crept forward, sometimes losing more than she gained, but always coming back for another attack at the crushing waves. There was something distinctly personal about the fight. It was man against nature. Everyone on the vessel was a part of the battle. I don't think I was frightened; no one seemed to be. All our minds and hearts and strength went out to help the *Albatross* when she staggered drunkenly after a smashing blow in the face.

Just as night closed in, lights showed on our port bow. An hour later the ship limped through the narrow entrance of the outer harbor of Keelung, battered and bruised but game to the last. Outside the typhoon roared past, increasing in violence every minute. Next morning during the half-hour run to the inner anchorage, the starboard engine gave way. Had that happened before we reached a shelter, nothing could have saved the ship. It required a week to make repairs in Keelung, and I collected diligently meanwhile. But it was unsatisfactory, for headhunting natives were only a short distance from the town, and the captain would not let me venture into the interior.

We stopped at Okinawa, where, at that time, many of the natives away from the coast had never before seen a white man, and went on to Nagasaki, Japan. There the voyage on the *Albatross* ended for me and a new and wholly different one began.

Whaling in Japan

A walk through the market at Nagasaki, the day after the *Albatross* arrived, may possibly have changed the whole current of my life. There I saw great chunks of whale meat on sale for food. I didn't know that shore whaling was being carried on in Japan, and I am sure no other naturalist did.

Pacific whales were virtually unknown, scientifically. If I
could stay there to study and collect specimens, it would
be a ten-strike. A cable to the museum gave enthusiastic approval.

The headquarters of the whaling company were at Shi-
moneski. I went there the next day. Nothing could have
been more cordial than my reception by the company officials. They were, they said, delighted to have an American scientist study at their stations, and I could have all
the skeletons the museum wanted. So I said farewell to my
shipmates on the *Albatross* while she started on her long
homeward voyage across the Pacific. A few days later I
was settled in a tiny Japanese hotel in the fishing village of
Ōshima.

The season was in full swing at Ōshima, and not a day
went by without at least one whale. Everything depended
upon getting the meat to market in the shortest possible time,
and the moment a whale arrived, men, women, and girls attacked it like vultures, cutting off huge chunks and load-
ing them on fast transports. There were no regular hours
and work never ceased until the last scrap of meat was on
its way to market.

Often whales arrived in the middle of the night. I always
went down to the wharf, not only to do my scientific work,
but to watch the strange scene. Flares of oil-soaked waste
lighted the station yard. Men and women, stripped to the
waist, girls and children in blue kimonos or skintight
breeches, waded through pools of shining blood, slipped
on the greasy blubber and tore like demons at masses of
steaming meat. "Ya-ra-cu-ra-so," they sang in a meaning-
less chant, as they strained and heaved at the colossal bones.

The scene was weird and unearthly, like a picture of the Eternal Pit with grinning devils at their business of torturing the ungodly.

I worked as hard as anyone, and longer hours, for after the blood and grease of the cutting platform had been washed off, my notes and measurements must be transcribed while they were fresh in mind. Seldom did I have more than five or six hours' sleep in any night. The problem of greatest scientific importance was to find out if the whales of the Atlantic and Pacific were the same or different species, and whether they migrated from one ocean to another. For future study I had to take photographs, descriptions, and about forty measurements of each specimen and send skeletons to the museum.

From Ōshima I moved to the village of Aikawa, in the north of Japan, where the whaling company had one of their largest stations. There I lived in a beautiful little doll's house overlooking the bay to a shore lined with twisted pine trees. The pines seemed incredibly old and tired of life, as though they had seen too much history since the days of the shoguns.

Fourteen little ships were operating out of the Aikawa station, and each carried a Norwegian gunner, for the Japanese had developed their industry under the tutelage of the Norwegians, in whose country shore-whaling first began. Most of them were fine men, rough but kindly, and I made many friends. I often went to sea on their vessels to study and photograph live whales, and in August I had an experience which came near to being the end of the road for me.

A Close Call

I was with a chap named Johnson, whom none of us liked, although he was one of the best gunners in Japan. We got fast to a big finback whale, but the harpoon struck between the shoulders and, as the bomb didn't explode, he was virtually uninjured. Dashing off like a hooked trout he took rope so fast that the brakes on the winch were smoking. Cable after cable were spliced together, and before his rush could be checked he had out nearly a mile of line. Then the brakes were set and he towed the ship forward with the engines going at full speed astern. After an hour of this, even his great strength began to fail. The rope was slowly reeled in, but as the ship dropped into the hollow of a swell, the line parted. A wild rush took him off again in a smother of foam. The chase dragged on for hours, but finally the gunner got fast with another harpoon.

"I'm afraid to pull him in," Johnson said. "I never saw such a strong whale. I'll send a boat out and lance him."

"Can I go?" I asked. "I'll pull one of the oars."

"All right. Take the *praam*."

A *praam* is a Norwegian boat big enough for three or four men which sits deep at the stern and can be spun around like a top. The Japanese mate carried a long, slender lance. A seaman and myself were at the oars. The whale lay at the surface, about a quarter of a mile away, now and then blowing lazily. As the tiny boat slipped up from behind, the body loomed bigger and bigger until to my excited eyes it seemed like a half-submerged submarine. Actually the whale was seventy-two feet long. Standing in the stern with lance poised, the mate steered us up right beside the beast.

"Way enough," he whispered.

Swinging the *praam* about, we backed up till the boat actually touched the body. Bracing himself, the little Japanese plunged the slender steel deep into the animal's lungs. As his arm went down, we gave a great heave on the oars. I heard a sickening crack, and my oar broke short off. The *praam* pivoted against the whale's side. The body lifted like a dripping mountain, and I saw the flukes, twenty feet across and weighing more than a ton, waving just above my head. They seemed to hang suspended for endless seconds and then, as in slow motion, to be coming down right on me. They missed my shoulder by a scant foot but caught the gunwale of the *praam*, splintering the side.

I was in the water, oilskins and boots pulling me down. My head struck wood as I came up, and instinctively I grabbed what remained of the boat. The mate was swimming toward the wrecked *praam*. The Jap sailor seemed to be stunned and lay face up beside the wreckage. In a moment he turned over and one hand groped blindly for a plank. The whale lay on its side, great clots of blood welling from the blowholes.

When my confused mind began to function, I saw a swarm of writhing blue-black bodies set upon the dying whale like a horde of vampires. Biting, tearing jaws gouged out chunks of flesh and blubber in a maelstrom of crimson froth. Others came, scores of sharks, following the blood trail. A blunt head bumped my foot and turned on its side, jaws open. I kicked and it backed off. Another slid close under my arm. I slugged it in the nose with my fist. Utterly terrified, I had just sense enough to yell at the mate to wrench off a

[185   ]

piece of the splintered boat and use it as a club. Each time a shark came too close, we jabbed it in the teeth or slammed its head.

One caught the toe of my rubber boot and hung on. I kicked frantically and the boot came off in its jaws. Crazed with the smell and taste of blood, the beasts were biting anything that moved. The mate fought like a madman, stabbing at the grinning faces, screaming in mortal fear. The Japanese sailor, still partly stunned, hung inert, his body half over the boat. A shark moved in, turned, and clamped its jaws on the calf of his leg. He shrieked in agony. The mate jabbed the shark in the eye, and the brute backed off astern with the chunk of bleeding human flesh sliding down its throat. The man slipped off the wreckage but I caught him by the hair and pulled him back across the *praam*. A few minutes later the ship passed us, Johnson bending over the gun. I yelled frantically, but he only waved his hand. He maneuvered the vessel deliberately, and fired a harpoon into the whale.

When the body finally sank in a smother of bloody foam and flashing fins, a *praam* put out from the ship. Two sailors picked us up. The mate was crying hysterically, but I felt only cold, murderous anger. Climbing up the ladder, I went forward to Johnson, still standing at the gun. He grinned happily.

"We got the whale, after all," he said. "I was afraid we'd lose him."

"Yes, and you left us to the sharks while you did it. Why?"

"The iron would have pulled out when we heaved him up. I had to get fast with another harpoon before he sank."

"You saw what was happening to us?"

"Sure, there were a few sharks about, but you were doing all right. You didn't have to worry."

For a moment I just stared. Then I blew up.

"Johnson, you're a god-damned, cold-blooded, inhuman son-of-a-bitch." I swung for his jaw, but he sensed what was coming and ducked. My fist grazed his cheek. The man looked at me as though I were an angry child.

"You're just mad," he said. "You'll get over it. Don't be silly."

Then he turned to stare down into the water, where the dim outlines of the dead whale showed just below the surface. What could one do with a man like that? He wasn't human! I left him and went below. The Japanese sailor lost his leg at the knee and Johnson lost his job. I never met him again. Reports indicated he had gone to the ice-filled waters of the Antarctic. That's where he belonged.

At the end of the summer, I sent the skeletons of four large whales to New York along with a dozen rare and unknown porpoises and two killer whales. It was an eighty-ton shipment. It gave the American Museum by far the finest collection of cetaceans in the world. Most of them hang today in the Hall of Ocean Life.

After more than a year and a half in the Orient, I reluctantly turned homeward via the Suez Canal. For several months I wandered over much of Europe, visiting all the principal museums and having small personal adventures with people and things. Not until my money was entirely gone, did I sail for New York. After paying tips on the ship and dock, I had exactly five cents left to take me on a street car to the American Museum.

[187]

Rediscovering an "Extinct" Whale

In Japan I had heard of a strange whale called the *koku kujira,* or "devil whale," which was being taken off the Korean coast during the winter on its southern migration. The description sounded much like the California gray whale that used to be killed in the lagoons of the Mexican shores before the Civil War. But the gray whale had been extinct for fifty years, so far as naturalists were aware. I thought a good deal about this devil whale on the way home. If I could go to Korea I might have the opportunity to rediscover a supposedly extinct species or find one new to science. Either prospect was intriguing. Moreover, the great forests of northern Korea up to Paik-to-San, the "Long White Mountain" on the Manchurian border, had never been visited by a white man. I had had considerable correspondence with Sir Francis Younghusband, the great Asiatic explorer, and he strongly urged me to do the job. It would, he said, be an exceedingly worthwhile piece of exploration. I could catch my whale during the winter and have the whole summer for the Korean expedition.

But it meant that I had to produce the money, for the American Museum could give me less than half. The Smithsonian Institution in Washington agreed to put up two thousand dollars if I sent them the skeleton of one of the whales. With my begging bowl in hand, I went to friends in New York and got an additional three thousand dollars.

So, a few days after the New Year in 1912, I sailed across the Japan Sea to the whaling station set in a picturesque bay among treeless, scrub-covered hills at Urusan, on the east coast of Korea. All the employees were Japanese, but

Koreans swarmed along the dock as the ship pulled in. That same night the station whistles roared out the call of whales. Flares appeared like magic, throwing a fitful light over the long dock and the black water of the harbor. In ten minutes I had pulled on my long boots and heavy coat. It was bitterly cold outside. The whaleship *Main*, shrouded in ice from stem to stern, swept proudly into the bay and slipped up to the crowded wharf. From her bow drooped the huge, black flukes of a whale. My great moment had come.

First glance showed that the flukes differed in shape from any that I had ever seen; also they were marked with strange gray circles. When the cutters hacked through the body and the posterior section came slowly into view, I saw that the back was finless and the dorsal edge strongly crenelated. Up came a wide, stubby flipper, then a short, arched head. These told the story. It was the "extinct" gray whale, beyond a doubt.

During the next six weeks I examined, measured, and photographed more than forty gray whales; saw them hunted; learned their clever tricks to avoid enemies; and pieced together, bit by bit, the story of their wanderings. The days at sea were bad — very bad. Always heavy weather and bitter cold, sleet and ice. Standing behind the harpoon gun for hours on end, my oilskins stiff from frozen spray, I used to curse the sea. But hardly was I back on shore, transcribing my wealth of new data, before the suffering was forgotten and I was keen to go out again.

A Horrible Show by the Killers

One day a herd of killer whales put on a fascinating, but horrible, show for us. Killers are the wolves of the sea and hunt in packs. Armed with four rows of tremendous teeth, they will literally devour a whale alive. We were chasing a gray whale about fifty feet long close inshore, where he was trying to escape by sliding behind rocks. Suddenly, the high dorsal fins of a pack of killers appeared, cutting the water like great black knives as the beasts rushed in. Completely disregarding our ship, the killers made straight for the gray whale. The beast, twice the size of the killers, seemed paralyzed with fright. Instead of trying to dive or get away, it turned on its back, flippers outspread, and lay motionless, awaiting its fate. A killer dashed up at full speed, forced its head into the whale's mouth by pressing against the lips, and ripped out great hunks of the soft, spongy tongue. Other killers were tearing at the throat and belly while the poor creature rolled in agony. I was glad when a harpoon ended its torture.

Briefly, the story of the lost gray whale is this. There are two separate herds and two separate migration routes from the Arctic Ocean. One is southward, along the American coast from the Bay of Alaska, where that herd spends the summer. The other, from the Okhotsk Sea, comes close along the Asiatic shore as far down as the Yellow Sea. Up to the time I went to Korea, scientists were unaware of the existence of the second route. The gray whale proved to be virtually a living fossil and one of the most important of all cetaceans.

When the station closed in March, two gray-whale skeletons had been boxed and shipped. Then I went up to Seoul to prepare for the expedition into the northern forests. I engaged a Japanese interpreter and a Korean cook. The Japanese spoke Korean like a native, but no English. That was all right, for I was fluent in Japanese by that time. The three of us departed on a tiny coastal vessel for the village of Sheshin on the east coast, not far south of Vladivostok.

The Long White Mountain

A hundred and fifty miles inland, I spent three weeks hunting a man-eating cave tiger that was terrorizing the countryside; then we pushed on to the edge of the wilderness. We had four Koreans and eight ponies. It was difficult to persuade the natives to go. Never having been beyond the point where a great swamp began in the forest, they were afraid we would be lost and die of starvation. My compass, of course, they could not understand.

The forest became denser at every mile. It was a pretty grim place. Time after time our ponies were mired and had to be pried out of the mud with poles. Lush ferns and rank grass made walking difficult. The trees were festooned with long streamers of gray moss, which formed a thick canopy overhead. Down where we were, there was only a gloomy half-light, occasionally shot through with patches of thin sun. I killed a bear on the fourth march, so we had fresh meat, but after that, for days, we did not see another sign of life. No sounds broke the utter stillness except the calls of the men. No birds or animals; not even a squirrel. To make matters worse, it began to rain. Not a hard refreshing rain, but a sullen drizzle which continued for a week.

The Koreans were completely disheartened, frightened at the gloomy stillness of the forest, and exhausted by strenuous work. They began to talk furtively among themselves and, when we camped, were ominously silent if I passed near their fire. The interpreter told me they were planning to desert with the ponies and food, leaving us to get back as best we could, or die. I estimated that we were not more than two days' march from the base of Paik-to-San. I told the men that we would soon reach the mountain; that I would give them double wages; further, that I would watch all night and if anyone touched a horse, he would be shot.

They didn't like it. My ultimatum was received in silence. The Japanese interpreter and I stood guard by turns through the night. Now and then one of the men got up to replenish the fire, but they made no move to leave camp. The next night was a repetition of the first. Both the interpreter and I were exhausted from lack of sleep and hard work. In the late afternoon we emerged into a wide burned track and the mountain rose majestically right in front of us. Banked to the top with snow, it looked like a great white cloud that had settled to earth out of the sky.

The beautiful mountain, and the open country, acted like magic on the Koreans. They began to talk and call to each other in laughing voices. I knew, then, that the crisis was over; they would not desert us. That night we camped at the base of Paik-to-San, well out in the burned area, beside a pond of snow water. The interpreter and I slept for fifteen hours utterly exhausted. In the late afternoon I shot a roe deer. The fresh meat completed the contentment of our party.

Four days at the Long White Mountain was sufficient. It was not important to climb to the summit. That had been done by Younghusband in 1879 when he came in from the Manchurian side. My object was to find what lay in the unknown Korean wilderness "over which I looked," Younghusband wrote, "with longing eyes." We had a compass line to the base of the mountain and a route map of the traverse.

Headwaters of the Yalu River

I determined not to return by the way we had come, but to strike through the forest to the headwaters of the Yalu River, which could not be far to the west. It was a tough trip; just about what we had experienced on the way to Paik-to-San. Dense forests, swamps, and drizzling rain. But the men pushed on with light hearts, laughing at difficulties and hard work, supremely confident that my little compass knew the way.

Finally, we camped on the bank of the great river, which, at that point, was only a rushing mountain torrent hardly a dozen yards across, and followed down its winding course to the first lumber camp, on the edge of Korean civilization. There, I sent back my men, loaded with silver and very happy. They were heroes to their people and capitalized on it to the ultimate degree.

The interpreter and I floated downstream on a huge log raft manned by Japanese. We lived in a little bark hut, slept in the sunshine, and watched the river widen and swell as it received the waters of a hundred tributaries. The trip was very restful after the weeks of strenuous work. We caught fish, shot ducks, and lived like kings. But a disreputable-looking person I was, dressed in Korean clothes and with my shoes almost gone, when we reached Antung, and the railroad, at the mouth of the Yalu River, on the east coast. The expedition had been eminently successful. The collection of mammals and birds, all from an unknown region, was extensive, and the exploration of the great forests was considered to be of importance by geographical societies.

In Seoul, I had the amusing experience of reading my own obituary. Because I was long overdue, some ambitious newspaper reporters had decided I was dead. That was widely publicized. There had been a memorial service for me in the Baptist church at Beloit, Wisconsin, where I was born. I learned from the reports what a really extraordinary guy I was before I died. But my cable to the museum brought an enthusiastic reply. Apparently the authorities were happy over my continued existence, and the results of the expedition. My parents, too, seemed to be glad about it.

For once, when I reached the museum at the end of 1912, after wandering in Russia and Scandinavia, I did not have plans for a new expedition. My graduate studies at Columbia University had been on a hit-or-miss basis; mostly miss, for I hadn't been able to "stay put" long enough to do much consecutive resident work. An anatomical study of the California gray whale would make an excellent thesis, so I plunged into it like a swimmer taking a dive in pleasant waters. Doing the monograph became almost as exciting as rediscovering the animal, and I worked at it day and night.

But in June of 1913, John Borden of Chicago asked me to go on his yacht, the *Adventuress*, to the Arctic to get a bowhead-whale skeleton, the only species the museum needed

[194   ]

to complete its collection of large cetaceans. The plan was sound, but the execution not so good. The *Adventuress* cruise to Alaska turned out to be little more than a big-game hunt. Kodiak bear, caribou, and mountain goats were on my list of animals, but no bowhead whale. The yacht couldn't get into the ice. Under ordinary conditions it would have been delightful, but I had come for a definite objective and was stymied by circumstances.

Shortly after World War I began in August, 1914, I married Yvette Borup, sister of George Borup, who had been a member of Peary's successful North Pole expedition. So many things were of immediate personal importance that, at first, the war seemed almost academic and very far away. It was Europe's quarrel and did not directly concern me. That, I think, was the attitude of most Americans in 1914-1915.

Land Explorations in China

I had decided to abandon the study of whales. The American Museum now had the largest and most complete collection of cetaceans in the world. It still has. I had obtained virtually all of them, written two extensive scientific monographs, a dozen or more shorter papers, and one popular book on whales. Professor Henry Fairfield Osborn, president of the museum, agreed that I was justified in turning to land exploration, which was what I had always intended to do eventually. Years ago he had predicted that Asia was the birthplace of primitive humans and the mother of much of the animal life of the world. His prophecy was based largely on theoretical grounds, for the interior of Asia was relatively unknown scientifically. Intensive exploration, designed to test his theory, would certainly yield important results.

I worked out a comprehensive plan for a series of expeditions to find out where was the best place for an attack on the main problem. Also, I had to train myself and learn the languages. Japanese I knew, and some Korean, but Chinese was essential. The first expedition would be a reconnaissance in Yunnan, the province in southwestern China bordering Tibet and Burma. It was a wild, mountainous region, imperfectly known geographically, and the fauna was virtually untouched. Professor Osborn was enthusiastic about the proposal, but there was the question of finances, as usual. The expedition would cost fifteen thousand dollars. The museum could donate only one third of that amount. Therefore, it was up to me to raise ten thousand dollars. Some of it came from my lectures and magazine writing; the rest was given by friends who were interested both in my work and in the museum. After two months of concentrated effort, I had pledges of more than ten thousand dollars. I chose Edmund Heller, who had been one of the naturalists with ex-President Theodore Roosevelt's African expedition, as the other scientist. In March, 1916, we sailed for Japan.

After spending a month hunting the so-called "blue tiger" in South China, we went up to Yunnan-fu, now known as Kunming, by way of the French railroad from Hanoi, Indochina. At Yunnan-fu a caravan of diminutive ponies carried us over the ancient Burma Road, which became famous in World War II, to Tali-fu in the center of the province. Thence, northward to the Tibetan frontier where, in secluded valleys, we found wild Moso tribesmen still using crossbows and poisoned arrows.

The mountains are stupendous. I remember particularly one day when we crossed a pass 16,000 feet high into the Yangtze River drainage basin. In a few hours we climbed out of the warm October sun into the dead of winter. Up through a larch forest and the higher belt of dwarf bamboo, beyond the uttermost tree line of rhododendrons, to the summit of the pass, bare and bleak and frozen. A bitter wind swirled about our tents. It was too cold to sleep. All night we shivered about a tiny fire, for there was little wood. Three of the ponies died from cold and the effects of the altitude. All of us suffered severely, and it was a miserable party that descended next morning into the golden sunshine of the October we had left so suddenly.

Every mountain range brought us into new valleys occupied by strange, aboriginal people. There are thirty distinct tribes in Yunnan, the remnants of the original inhabitants of China. Just as the white man pushed the American Indians westward, so did the Chinese drive the aborigines south and west, centuries ago. Now they are concentrated in the mountains of Yunnan. One of the tribes, the Lolos, never had been subdued by the Chinese. They still occupied a territory in western China called "Lolo Land," where no Chinese was allowed to pass.

Natives Who Had Never Seen a White Man

Small bands of Lolos had wandered from the forbidden country and settled in Yunnan. After crossing a pass, we came suddenly upon a Lolo village hidden away in a deep valley. Fine, tall fellows they were, with long heads, high-bridged noses, and thin lips; almost a Caucasian type of face. They had never seen a white man, and at first were militantly on the defensive. Tobacco and small presents soon made them realize that we were friends.

Everything about us was interesting to them. Cameras, watches and the like were too far beyond their comprehension to be impressive, but the field glasses seemed a miracle; also, my high-powered rifle and revolver were tools of a god, for their own guns were primitive matchlock things with a range of only thirty yards. In photographs they could not recognize themselves. It was only by pointing to some special article of dress, and indicating it in the photograph, that they could be made vaguely to understand.

Through the mountains, up to the frontier of Tibet, we went, finding new mammals and birds, new plants, new tribes, and unmapped country. We crossed the Yangtze River, there less than fifty yards wide, into a gloomy chasm through which no white man had ever passed. Then down the Mekong River valley and southward into the steaming tropics of the Burma border. Thick jungle, palm trees, and smothering vegetation instead of snow-capped peaks! Leopard, tiger, sambur deer, and monkeys; cobras, pythons, jungle fowl, and beautiful silver pheasants. A country as different from that we had left as Borneo is from Alaska!

The Salween River lay between us and civilization at Bhamo, on the Irrawaddy River in northern Burma. I wanted to go to the Salween valley but wondered if it was worth the risk. A ghastly place it is, deserted of all human life, given over to peacocks, leopards, and wild red dogs. Even the aboriginal Lisos dared not face the malignant malaria which makes the valley a fever-stricken hell.

It was there that General Stilwell's Chinese troops fought the Japanese during World War II. In a copy of *Time* magazine, December 7, 1942, I read such a vivid description of the Salween River valley that I am quoting it here:

Dying weather. Mountains, mottled green, yellow, red and gray, tower thousands of feet into the air, and drop precipitously into the emerald green Salween, called by the natives *Wu-ti-ho*, the "River without a Bottom." In the jungles with the Chinese, were leopards and tigers, pythons that swallowed whole live hogs, monkeys that stole man's food, wolves that howled at night and tried to eat dead soldiers. In the river, said the natives, were little fish with hides thicker than leather; bigger leather-skinned fish whose mouths opened and shut like folding doors. Some of the natives, ceremoniously neutral, stalked the Japanese with poisoned arrows; some hunted the heads of unwary Chinese.

But worst of all was the *ta-paitzu* (malaria). This was the worst malaria spot in the world. Deadly mosquitoes infested the gorge. Exhausted, underfed and ragged soldiers had neither mosquito nets for protection, nor quinine to combat the fever. Casualties from malaria were higher than from combat. Apparently well men, trudging along the mountain passes, would suddenly flush, complain of the fire in their heads, then die. It was months before adequate doses of quinine reached them.

The Deadly Salween Valley

We were taking a big risk, but I decided to go to the Salween, for no naturalist had ever been there and whatever mammals we obtained would certainly be new to science. There were gloves, head nets, and mosquito covers for every man and every tent. I was prepared to give deep injections of quinine, which was then the only way to successfully battle the fever. So we went, and remained ten days. Our reward was a fine collection of mammals, and I was the only one who contracted fever. I had lost a glove and the mosquitoes bit my hand while I was lying in wait for peacocks on the river's edge. That night I was shot full of quinine and next day we climbed gratefully five thousand feet, out of the poison valley to the healthy ridges where we could look down upon the river winding like a thin, green line below. For three days I shook with chills and burned as though there were fire in my blood, but quinine brought me through. Strangely enough, the malaria germs lay dormant in my blood until five years ago, when they came to life; they have bothered me periodically ever since.

There were hunts for monkeys, goral, serow, sambur, and leopard before we were back again on the Burma Road, working slowly southward to Bhamo and civilization. For nine months we had been wandering in the wilderness to bring out the biggest collection ever taken in Asia on a single expedition. There was a complete route map, 2100 mammals and 1000 birds, besides many fish, reptiles, and batrachians, all from regions where no collector, and few white men, had ever before set foot.

In Bhamo, for the first time in many months, we had

news of the outside world and heard that the United States had declared war on Germany. Now that America was in the struggle, I felt a tremendous urge to get home and into the show. But that was easier said than done. We had to go two thirds around the world on any ship that would take us. I was frantic with impatience.

At very long last we reached New York with all our collections, and the day after Christmas my first son was born. He was named George Borup Andrews, for his explorer uncle. Immediately after George's birth, I went to Washington to offer my services, and a week later was on the way back to China in Naval Intelligence, bound specifically for Peking.

In China During the War

Peking remained my headquarters all through the war period, but it was not a static existence for me. My peregrinations took me over much of China and Manchuria; twice across the Gobi Desert from Kalgan, the frontier city north of Peking, to Urga, the capital of Mongolia, and northward, on horseback, through the vast forests into Siberia. Urga, when taken over by the Soviets, was renamed Ulan Bator, the "Red City." The traveling fitted perfectly into my peacetime job of Asiatic exploration, and I viewed each country from the standpoint of the great expedition which now had taken definite form in my mind.

Always time was of the utmost importance, so when I crossed the Gobi it was by motor car. Only two or three years earlier, the first automobile had been driven over the ancient caravan trail to Urga, fighting rocks and sand and mud, but getting through. Instead of lurching back and forth between the humps of a camel for two months, one could do the journey in a car in five to seven days — if he were lucky.

The first time I went to Urga was in early August, when Mongolia is at its best. Warm sunlit days and fresh cold nights! It was an interesting trip, and not only because of the scenery. Mongolia was not at war with anyone, so the only human danger we expected was from the perennial Chinese bandits in the cultivated area a hundred miles north of Kalgan. The second day took us out of that, and we drove peacefully along a hard trail just over the frontier of Outer Mongolia. My companion, Charles Coltman, was asleep in the back seat of the open car when we came to Ude, where a rocky promontory juts out into the plain. Suddenly five men appeared on the outcrop and opened fire. Why, I don't know, but the bullets were zinging above our heads and plunking into the car every second. Charlie woke up with a yell, frantically pulling our rifles out of the cases. Humped over the wheel, I zigzagged back and forth across the trail, but the lead still kept coming. It was good shooting — too damned good.

"God a'mighty, Charlie," I shouted, "they'll kill us. Pass me my rifle."

I leaned back to take the gun and, at that split second, a bullet shattered the whole lower side of the steering wheel, right where my body had been pressed. It couldn't have been a narrower squeak. That bullet just wasn't marked with my name.

The trail led around a high wall of rock into the sandy bed of a dry stream. The car stalled in three minutes, but at least we were out of sight of whoever it was that was trying to kill us. Doubtless, they knew we'd be stuck there; all autos were. Leaving the motor running we climbed the rocks and peeped over the top. The five men stood in plain sight. Probably they were Mongol bandits wanting to collect a motor car.

Pretty soon our potential murderers started to climb down the cliff, evidently bent on finishing off what they had begun. But we weren't having it that way. Charlie selected one fellow silhouetted against the sky. I lined my sights on another, just in front. At the crash of our rifles, Charlie's client sat down suddenly and rolled over. Mine did a magnificent swan dive right off the cliff. The other three ducked back among the rocks. It must have been a bit of a surprise to them, for I guess they thought we didn't have guns since we had not returned their fire. That night when we reached a big lama temple, I couldn't resist burning a couple of *joss* sticks in front of the god who grinned so benevolently upon us.

Urga, a City Out of the Past

Three days later we arrived in Urga, during a night black as the pit, and slept in the *yurt* of a Mongol duke, Loobitsan. When I went outside in the morning to douse my face in cold water, by some miracle time and space seemed to have been obliterated, and I was back in a settlement of western America during the Indian-fighting days. Every house was surrounded by high stockades of unpeeled logs, and, in an open space by itself, just where it ought to be for proper defense, was the blockhouse. (I learned later that it enclosed a lama temple.) Larch trees straggled down almost to the village edge. They came from the unbroken reaches of the virgin forest stretching away in a vast rolling sea of green far beyond the Siberian border. The picture only needed a befeathered Indian, or a buckskin-clad frontiersman emerging from the woods with a deer slung across his back.

The second time I crossed the Gobi was with a Czech courier, in the dead of winter on the heels of a blizzard. The temperature stood at fifty degrees below zero and we reached Urga so nearly frozen that it seemed the cold had cut into the very marrow of our bones. Then we had to ride northward through the forest into Siberia on horseback. It was a bitter experience. Three of my companion's fingers were frozen and had to be amputated. But even at their worst, the country and the people fascinated me. Here was where I would make my scientific attack on Central Asia. Mongolia, it seemed, held all the answers, but I must know it more intimately. I must ride over the desert on camel and horseback and live as the Mongols live. So, since when the war ended I was still in Peking, I raised enough money by letter among my friends in New York to return for five months.

The summer passed all too quickly, and I started back to China in a motor car, but almost didn't get there. The first night we camped on the plain a mile from a lama monastery. The tiny houses of five thousand priests cluster about three temples. Also, there are dogs — hundreds of them! Great shaggy fellows like the Tibetan mastiff! They slink about the place waiting for scraps and the bodies of dead lamas.

As a result of the diet of human flesh, every person is **a** potential meal to the Mongol dogs.

Nearly Eaten by Dogs

After a dinner of antelope steak, we spread our fur bags on the ground and went to sleep. Two loaded rifles were between us; one a tiny .22-caliber Winchester and the other a 6.5-mm. Mannlicher. During the night my companion was restless, and at two o'clock sat up suddenly, wide-awake. There, circling about us in the moonlight, was a pack of fourteen dogs. To them we were dead Mongols ready to be eaten. A scream brought me up just as they dashed in. Half awake, I grabbed the first rifle my hand touched, and fired blindly. It happened to be the .22-caliber Winchester, but the little bullet must have caught the big leader in the head for he sank in his tracks, stone dead. The pack swerved, swept by only a few yards away, and I fired twice more, hitting two other dogs. Instantly there was a blood-curdling chorus of yelps and growls as the wounded animals were devoured alive. I dragged the dead leader far beyond our camp, and the next morning all that remained of his carcass were a few bits of bloody hair. Outside Urga, one day, I watched a pack of dogs tear apart the corpse of a Mongol. It disappeared in seven minutes!

Back in Peking I took account of stock. The summer had brought the museum a collection of fifteen hundred mammals from a region where they had not had a single specimen. That was the obvious payoff for the time and money. But most important was the knowledge I had gained of the Gobi as a theater of work for my great expedition. It would be unlike any that had been done before; it would initiate a new type of exploration. Every detail was clear in my mind, and I could hardly wait to get back to America.

Three days after reaching New York I lunched with Professor Osborn in the president's office at the museum. To me, he filled the same role as a sponsor that Morris K. Jesup, the museum's former president, did for Admiral Peary. The professor knew I had something important on my mind. When coffee had been served, and we were smoking comfortably, he said, "Now, let's have it. It's another expedition, I suppose."

"Yes, that's why I came back. The expedition I talked to you about years ago, before I went to Yunnan. To test your theory of Central Asia as a center of origin for world animal life. Especially to try to find evidence of primitive man. Mongolia is the place."

"Well," said the president, "how do you propose to go about it?"

I began talking. In two minutes Professor Osborn's eyes were glowing. He stopped smoking and just sat there looking hard at me and absorbing every word.

"More than that, we should try to reconstruct the whole history of the Central Asian plateau; its geology, fossils, past climate and vegetation. We've got to collect its living mammals, birds, fish, reptiles, insects, and plants and map the unexplored parts of the Gobi. Intensive exploration of a new kind, bringing to bear half a dozen sciences *in the field* on a single problem. The specialists will help each other interpret correctly what they find *as they find it*. The biggest land expedition ever to leave the United States."

"Of course," said he, "it's a gamble so far as fossils are concerned. The Russians never found anything in Mongolia. What makes you think you can do better?"

"Because their past work has been too much political and too little scientific. There have been a few good men — Prjevalski, Kozlov, Obrechev — but they had to produce economic or political results. Science never was the primary aim of any of the Russian expeditions. Even their map is so inaccurate as to be almost useless. Moreover, they all used camels. They could only average ten miles a day. We'll have motor cars. We can go a hundred miles a day, if my estimate is right, so we ought to do in one season as much as the others did in ten. Instead of spending the winter as they did, and almost perishing from cold, we'll return each autumn."

"How do you know you can use motor cars in the desert?"

"I don't *know* it. But I believe from all I have seen of the country that it can be done. It will be largely a matter of preparation. The terrain is mostly fine gravel. I don't think there is much loose sand. We must have every conceivable motor part, and experts who can almost build a new car if necessary. Such men exist. I can get them."

"How are you going to supply your cars with gasoline? You can't carry enough to go very far."

"We will have a supporting caravan of camels. It will act exactly like the supply ship to a fleet at sea. The camels must leave months ahead of us during the winter, and we'll meet them at a rendezvous six or seven hundred miles out in the desert. They will carry gasoline, food, and most of our equipment and bring out the specimens."

"What about your scientific staff?" asked the professor. "How do you intend to work?"

"We must have the best men in the world representing all the sciences that will help us solve our problems."

"But," said Professor Osborn, "you probably can't all work together in the same place at the same time."

"I've thought of that. There will be three or four units, each complete and able to maintain itself independently for at least a fortnight. The main camp will be the base, and each party will work out from there."

The professor asked many more questions. Finally he said, "We've got to do it. The plan is scientifically sound. Moreover, it grips the imagination. Finances are the only obstacle. You estimate five years for the expedition and a quarter of a million dollars. That's a lot of money and there is a severe business depression at present. Of course, the museum will do all it can, but that won't be much in the way of cash. Getting the money will be up to you. What are your ideas on that score?"

"My best chance, I believe, is to make it a 'society expedition' with a big 'S.' You know how New York society follows a leader. If they have the example of someone like Mr. J. P. Morgan, for instance, they'll think it is a 'must' for the current season."

"Yes," said the professor thoughtfully, "it might work. Anyway it's worth trying and I think the best way. Moreover, this is big enough to be interesting to those people who are accustomed to think only of big things."

"Then if it's all right with you, I'll get to work at once — tomorrow."

The professor smiled. "In spite of all the difficulties, I'm sure you *can* do it. Who are you going to see first?"

"Mr. Morgan," I said. "If he is interested, I'm sure of the others."

Financing the Central Asiatic Expedition

Mr. J. P. Morgan was first vice-president of the museum, and I had known him for some years. The next day I telephoned him at the bank and asked for an interview.

"Where do you want to see me? At my house or here?" he asked.

"At your house; preferably after a good breakfast."

"That sounds ominous," he laughed, "but come to my library at nine o'clock tomorrow morning."

I went, and was ushered into the study of the beautiful library. In a moment Mr. Morgan strode through the door. I rose to greet him, and he said with a smile, "Well, Roy, what do you want? Money?"

"Yes, I do, but not unless you're really interested."

"I'm interested in everything. I suppose it's another expedition. Tell me about it."

I unfolded a map and we bent over it together. There is always something exciting about a map, and that was particularly true in those days, thirty years ago, when a lot of blank areas were still marked "unexplored." Much of the Central Gobi was a white space, with only the few thin lines of ancient caravan trails weaving uncertainly across it. I launched into my story with the enthusiasm of a fanatic.

In two minutes everything was forgotten except the prospect of what could be done if only I had the money. Mr. Morgan listened with rapt attention. Two or three times he interrupted with questions.

I told him, too, of my plan for a new type of intensive exploration and the possibilities of rapid transport with motor cars. At the end of fifteen minutes I stopped, breathless. Mr. Morgan swung about with his eyes aglow.

"It's a great idea, a great idea. I'll gamble with you. How much money do you need?"

"A quarter of a million dollars and five years at the very least, Mr. Morgan."

"All right, I'll give you fifty thousand. Now you go out and get the rest of it."

"That's wonderful. I'll surely get it. There is, I suppose, no use asking who of your friends might be interested?"

"No, I couldn't tell you that. But — hold on — Albert Wiggin! He sent a man to me last week. It cost me ten thousand. You go to him, tell him I sent you, and that he'll do damn well to shell out."

I didn't know Mr. Wiggin, who was president of the Chase National Bank, but I called his secreatry, asked for an appointment, and said I had a message for him from Mr. Morgan.

A few days later I was ushered into his office. Mr. Wiggin sat behind a glass-topped desk and I was interested to see that there wasn't a paper on it; only an ink stand, a blotter, and two pens. We chatted for a moment and then the banker said:

"My secretary told me you had a message from Mr Morgan. May I ask what it is?"

I smiled. "Shall I give it to you in his exact words?"

"Yes, of course."

"I'm trying to finance a great expedition to Central Asia, and Mr. Morgan has given me fifty thousand dollars. He told me to come to you, say he sent me, and that you'd do 'damned well to shell out.'"

Mr. Wiggin slapped his desk and laughed, albeit ruefully:

"Damn it all. That would be the chap I sent to him last week. Well, tell me about the expedition."

I got out my map and started, but it was obvious Mr. Wiggin wasn't much interested. So I cut it short and rose to go after five minutes.

"Very exciting, very exciting," he said. "I'll send you a check in a few days." He did, but it wasn't for ten thousand!

The late Arthur Curtis James, holder of more railroad securities than any other man in the world, was next on my list. Mr. James was one of our trustees and I had met him frequently at the museum. He was a gruff, bearded man, owner of the beautiful sailing yacht the *Aloha*. I told him once that he impressed me as a sailor, not a financier, and I think he liked that, for the sea and sailing ships were his passion. His secretary gave me an appointment, but she picked a bad time.

At nine o'clock in the morning I went into his office in the Phelps-Dodge Corporation. Mr. James was hopping mad. He had just read a letter from Professor Osborn asking for a contribution to the museum's deficit of seventy-five thousand dollars. As I came in the door Mr. James, without any preliminary greeting, roared:

"Here's a letter from your president. He says he knows

[211]

I'd 'enjoy' contributing to the deficit! *Enjoy* contributing to the deficit! I can't think of anything I'd *enjoy* less! There shouldn't be a deficit. He ought to spend his income and no more. Damn bad policy. I'm going to get off the board if he uses his trustees just as checkbooks."

There didn't seem to be much that I could say, since the museum's finances were not my responsibility.

"I'm sorry, Mr. James. I seem to have caught you at the wrong time. I was going to talk about an expedition to Central Asia, but I guess it had better wait."

"No, no, you're here. Go ahead. What's it all about?"

I began rather lamely, I'm afraid, for it was a tough spot. I couldn't capture his interest, and his eyes were still snapping with anger. Finally he broke in:

"How much am I going to be stuck for this expedition?"

That made *me* mad.

"Mr. James, you're not going to be stuck a damn cent. This isn't something the trustees are doing as a body. I came to you as an individual. If you aren't interested, I don't want your money. You are busy, and so am I. Good morning."

I got to my feet, reached for my hat, and started out the door. The anger went out of his eyes like turning off a switch. He had never called me by my first name before, but he said:

"Now, now, Roy, I'm sorry. I shouldn't have ripped out at you like that. I can't let you go off to China being sore at me. Will ten thousand do you any good?"

"I'll say it will! I hadn't expected that much."

"Well, you can have it and welcome. Teach me not to lose my temper. Always have to pay for it when I get mad."

I walked out of the Phelps-Dodge offices in a daze. Raising money from the world's greatest financiers surely was a strange business! One gave it to me because it was the pay-off for another, and now I had ten thousand by getting mad and making a man ashamed of his own temper. Talk about adventures in the Gobi Desert! Adventures in Wall Street were just as exciting and more incomprehensible.

My original idea that the expedition could be financed by making it "the thing to do" of society for that winter proved to be 100 per cent right. A dinner and reception given by the then Mrs. Willard Strait (the former Dorothy Whitney), at which I showed Mongolian lantern slides, started a flood of invitations. Night after night, I donned white tie and tails and talked Gobi Desert at some one of New York's great houses. Professor Osborn was a staunch supporter. He gave the benefit of his great scientific and social prestige, and introductions to many prominent people. I haunted Wall Street, spoke at luncheons, went to teas, gave public lectures in the evenings, wrote four magazine articles and a book. There never was a moment of relaxation. Compared to the financial battle, fieldwork was child's play. But I had known what it would be like before it started. Peary, and all the other important explorers, had gone through the same ordeal. It was the price one had to pay.

The "Missing Link" Expedition

With a gift of fifty thousand dollars from Mr. John D. Rockefeller, Jr., the expedition's funds reached the two-hundred-thousand-dollar mark, and I felt it was time for a public announcement of our plans. Twenty-one reporters were present at the news conference. It made the front page of every New York newspaper and was cabled all over the world. I was, however, greatly disturbed because the press stressed the search for early human remains, rather than the broader aspects of the exploration we hoped to make. But there was nothing we could do about it. In a week we were known as "The Missing Link Expedition."

Immediately applications to join poured in by mail, telegrams, and personal visits. The number reached ten thousand, including three thousand from women. Two secretaries had their hands full. The tempo of my activities increased to the point that four or five hours' sleep any night was the maximum. But when we were ready to sail for China, in March, 1921, the quarter of a million dollars had been subscribed, the staff selected, and the vast amount of equipment shipped. The fact that we had the personal blessings of the President of the United States and of the Secretary of State was an added satisfaction. I was almost a nervous wreck, but the first part of the job was done. It only remained to make good in the field.

I may say that I had to have the courage of my convictions as to the use of motor cars in the desert. No one else thought it could be done. There were dire predictions that if we ever returned, it would be on camel back. No company would insure our cars against total loss. Even Lloyd's of London turned us down.

We could not, of course, go to Mongolia that first summer. There was too much preliminary work to be done. First, I had to find a suitable house as headquarters for the expedition; arrange the complicated diplomatic negotiations for our work with the Chinese and Mongol governments; buy camels, hire a native staff, get food and equipment packed, and start the caravan during the winter so that it might meet our motor party six hundred miles out in the desert.

All of these things were accomplished eventually, and April 17, 1922, we left Peking for Kalgan, the gateway to the great plateau, on the first expedition into Mongolia. At last the years of preparation, the months of strain and worry were ended. The fieldwork had begun. It is impossible to give more than a few incidents of those exciting months in the desert, but certain pictures stand out in my mind with photographic clearness. One is of the day when we found the first fossils. That I shall never forget. At a promising-looking exposure of yellow gravel on the edge of a great basin filled with camel-sage, I dropped Drs. Berkey, Granger, and Morris.

"You," I said, "stop here and have a look. I'll make camp five miles away where the caravan should have left us a dump of gasoline."

The tents were pitched at the base of a low gray-white ridge. While I was watching a sunset which splashed the sky with gold and red, the geologists' cars roared into camp. I knew something unusual had happened, for no one said a word, but Walter Granger's eyes were shining. He was the chief paleontologist. Silently he dug into his pocket and produced a handful of bone fragments; out of his shirt came a titanothere's tooth and the various folds of his clothes yielded other fossils. Drs. Berkey and Morris, geologists, were loaded in a like manner. Walter stuck out his hand:

[215   ]

"Well, Roy, we've done it. The stuff is here. We picked up fifty pounds of bone in an hour."

Then we all laughed and shouted and shook hands and pounded one another on the back and did all the things men do when they are very happy. No prospector ever examined the washing of a gold pan with greater interest than we handled that little heap of fossil bones. Rhinoceros we were sure of and titanotheres, *but no titanotheres had ever before been discovered outside of America.* The other specimens were of smaller animals not positively identifiable.

The First Dinosaur

While dinner was being cooked, Granger wandered off along the gray-white outcrop that lay like a recumbent reptile west of camp. Even in the failing light he found a half-dozen fossil bones. We realized that there was another deposit at our very door. The next morning, just as I was starting out to shoot, Dr. Berkey returned to camp. For the distinguished professor of geology of Columbia University, he was acting very queerly, but he would give me no information.

"Come with me," was all he said.

When we reached the summit of the outcrop, I saw Granger on his knees working at something with a camel-hair brush.

"Take a look at that and see what you make of it," said Berkey. I saw a great bone, beautifully preserved, outlined in the rock. There was no doubt. It was dinosaur.

"It means," said Dr. Berkey, "that we are standing on Cretaceous strata of the Age of Reptiles — *the first Cretaceous strata, and the first dinosaur, ever discovered in Asia north of the Himalaya Mountains."*

Unless one is a scientist, it is difficult to appreciate the importance of that discovery. It meant that we had added an entirely new geological period to the knowledge of the continental structure of Central Asia, and had opened a paleontological vista of dazzling brilliance. With the rhinoceros and titanothere teeth, the dinosaur leg bone was the first indication that the theory upon which we had organized the expedition might be true: that Asia is the mother of the life of Europe and America.

A few days later we met our caravan, which had started in the dead of winter, months before we left Kalgan in the motor cars. The rendezvous was to be at a well called Turin. It was at the root of an ancient mountain, ages ago of majestic height, but now reduced by wind and weather to a ragged mass of granite rising like a timeworn citadel above the plain. We came to the base of the "mountain" at noon, and in the distance saw a great caravan camped beside the trail. Soon we could make out the American flag streaming from one of the loads. Merin, the Mongol leader, said they had arrived only an hour before we came. *This was the day on which I had told Merin, months earlier, to reach Turin.* All through the expedition the synchronization of the cars and the caravan worked extraordinarily well, and just as had been planned.

We camped in the center of the mountain, on a grassy plain, with orders for the caravan to follow. I climbed to a flat-topped ledge of granite just as the great, white leading camel, bearing the American flag, appeared from behind a boulder in the rocky gateway. Majestically, in single file,

[217   ]

the animals advanced among the rocks and strung out in a seemingly endless line. My blood thrilled at the sight. The camels swung past the tents, broke into three files like soldiers, and knelt to have their loads removed; then with the usual screams and protests, they scrambled to their feet and wandered down the hill-slope to the plain, nibbling at the vegetation as they went.

For more than a month in the early spring, sandstorms made our lives miserable. An entry in my *Journal* on June 14th tells of what we often had to face, until July brought heat and mirage:

There had been a gentle breeze but suddenly it dropped to a dead calm; a heavy stillness, vaguely depressing. Slowly I became conscious that the air was vibrating to a continuous even roar, louder every second. Then I understood. One of the terrible desert storms was on the way. The shallow basin seemed to be smoking like the crater of a volcano. Yellow "wind devils" eddied up and swirled across the plain. To the north, an ominous tawny bank advanced at racehorse speed. I started back toward camp, but almost instantly a thousand shrieking storm demons were pelting my face with sand and gravel. Breathing was difficult; seeing impossible. I reached the rim of the basin, and tried to strike diagonally toward the tents. Even the ground beneath my feet was invisible. In perhaps ten minutes, perhaps half an hour, I stumbled into a depression and lay there trying to think. Suddenly forms took shape in the smother right beside me. I reached out and caught one of them by the leg. They were three of the men. Pressing our mouths close against each other's ears, we held a consultation. One thought the tents were directly south of us. I had no idea where they were. Clinging together, we groped our way through the blinding murk. At last we stumbled over a black object. It was the cook tent, still standing, but with every blast in danger of being torn to shreds. We felt our way inside and lay on the ground, our faces buried in wet cloths; it was the only way we could breathe.

The gale continued for an hour and then suddenly came a soundless calm. Not a breath of air stirred the American flag which hung limply above the mess tent, whipped almost to ribbons. The silence was uncanny after the roar and rush of the storm. Peace lasted for only a short time; then the wind began again and developed into a full gale. For two weeks it blew almost without ceasing, until our nerves were worn and frayed. But we knew that some time it would end and give place to the hot, sunlit days when a breeze would be very welcome.

Discovering the World's Largest Mammal

August 4th was one of the high spots of the first expedition, for that afternoon Walter Granger discovered parts of a *Baluchitherium*, the "Beast of Baluchistan." It was the most gigantic mammal that ever walked upon the earth, but had been described only from three vertebrae and some foot bones from Baluchistan, Pakistan. No one knew what sort of creature it was. Now the mystery could be dispelled. Few discoveries in paleontology have been more exciting.

Granger had recovered the end of the humerus, or upper foreleg bone, and one side of the lower jaw with teeth as large as apples. This was fine as far as it went, but what we needed most of all was a skull. We talked until late that night. I went to sleep with my mind full of *Baluchitherium,* and had a vivid dream of discovering the animal's skull. Although Granger was sure he had found all the bones that were exposed, I determined to go back to the place and make a further search. With Shackleford and a Chinese chauffeur, Wang, we returned to "Wild Ass Camp" after tiffin. The two other men prospected in the bottom of a gully, while I inspected the side, now and then sticking my pick into a bit of discolored earth. In about five minutes I reached the summit of the ridge, and looked down the other side. A fragment of bone projecting out of the bottom of the wash caught my eyes. Its color was unmistakable. With a yell, I leaped down the steep slope. When Shack and Wang came around the corner on the run, I was on my knees, scratching like a terrier. Already a large chunk of bone had been unearthed and a dozen fragments were visible in the sand. They were beautifully fossilized and so hard we had no fear of breaking them. Laughing in hysterical excitement we made the sand fly as we took out piece after piece of bone.

Suddenly my fingers struck a huge block. Shack followed it down to the other end; then he produced a tooth. My dream had come true! It was the skull of a *Baluchitherium.* At six o'clock, while the men were having tea, we burst into camp, shouting like children. Granger had made so many important discoveries in his paleontological career that he was not easily stirred, but our story brought him up standing. He was as excited as the rest of us.

Even though we realized the "Baluch" was a colossal beast, the size of the bones left us astounded. It was a giant among giants. When those remains, and others that we found later, were studied in the museum by Professor Osborn, he pronounced the animal to be a great hornless rhinoceros. It stood seventeen feet high at the shoulders, twenty-four feet in body length, had a long neck, stilted limbs, and probably prehensile lips adapted to feeding on the herbage of the higher tree branches, like a giraffe. A six-foot man could easily have walked beneath the belly. The "Baluch" lived during the Oligocene Period, about thirty-five or forty million years ago, and was so highly specialized that when the climate and vegetation changed, it could not adapt itself and became extinct without ever leaving Central Asia.

Another memorable day of the first expedition was when Walter Granger and I stood on the summit of an unnamed peak in the Altai Mountains. As far as our eyes could reach, the country was unexplored, a great white space on the Russian map. We looked over a vast panorama of rolling, yellow plains cut by ravines and gullies. From the mountain's base, enormous alluvial fans spread emerald carpets out of gloomy canyons, to a line of sand dunes along the edge of a desert lake. Far to the north, an extraordinary red mesa capped with black lava, like chocolate frosting on a gigantic cake, ran through the center of a long, narrow valley.

We went there next day, entering by a rocky gateway. Across the southern end of the valley, a wall of lava blocks stretched for half a mile in a serpentine line. Our archaeologist said it had been made by some pre-Mongol people, many centuries ago. The eastern end of the valley broke off abruptly into a wild chaos of ravines and chasms. The fantastic shapes gave our camp an atmosphere of unreality.

We seemed to be living in the world of a long-dead yester-day. At any moment dinosaurs might wander to the door-ways of our tents from out of the vast red canyons! One of the men did find the skeleton of a dinosaur completely turned to iron. It lay in a block of hematite, partly exposed, but could not be removed. That was all the more tantaliz-ing, for it represented a type quite unknown to science.

It was on August 30th that from this camp we started eastward toward the Well of the Sweet Water, crossed the "mountains" that did not exist, and discovered the Flam-ing Cliffs, where seventy million years ago, the dinosaurs had laid their eggs.

Back in Peking

Late in September we drove through the narrow streets of Kalgan, our cars covered with the yellow dust of the Gobi, with cutouts open and blaring horns. From the doors of every shop people rushed out, lined the streets, and cheered to welcome us home. They had expected never to see us again when we drove away more than five months before.

That night Walter Granger and I tried to sleep on a soft bed in a stuffy room. We tossed and turned and smoked cig-arette after cigarette. Sleep wouldn't come. Finally Walter said:

"Hell, Roy, it's this damned bed. Let's get our sleeping bags and bunk outside." We stole out like thieves, unrolled our fur bags on the earth of a defunct flower bed, looked up at the stars for a few minutes while the wind caressed our faces, and dropped into a dreamless sleep.

The day after reaching Peking, the staff gathered in our headquarters to draft a cable to the American Museum outlining our discoveries. When we came to take stock of the season's work, it was surprising to realize how much had been accomplished in every branch of science. The method of correlated studies had initiated a new era of intensive scientific exploration. We were well started upon an ambitious topographical program — making a new and accurate map of Mongolia. Moreover, the combined motor and camel transport had given ten times the efficiency of previous explorers in the Gobi, as I thought it would. Our cars had covered three thousand miles and all were fit to go again.

After the first telegram, we had sessions with the foreign newspaper correspondents. Congratulatory dispatches poured in. Professor Osborn cabled: "You have written a new chapter in the history of life upon the earth." Messages came from scientific and geographical societies in many parts of the world: America, England, Australia, France, Germany, Hungary, Denmark, and Sweden. It was satisfactory to say the least. Moreover, we had had an experience that never again could come to any living man, for the Central Asian plateau was the last great region in the world so nearly unknown, scientifically. Almost everything was new: the mammals, reptiles, fish from the desert lakes, the geology, and particularly the fossils.

Incidentally, we had opened a vast region for commercial motor transportation. Representatives of Chinese importing firms asked how they could go in cars to various points in the Gobi to bring out valuable furs, contract with the natives for hides, camels' and sheep's wool, and ponies. By the end of our second expedition, three or four cars were using the trails we had mapped. There were many others in succeeding years. It was a striking example of how quickly commerce follows on the heels of exploration. Interesting, too, was the fact that half a dozen companies now were eager to insure our cars against total loss.

Since the first expedition was in the nature of reconnaissance, we prepared for the second year with a larger staff. Some of the men returned to America for the winter and others remained to carry on explorations in various parts of China. Exactly twelve months after our first expedition we left Peking again for the Gobi. There had been an unprecedented number of robberies along the camel trail north of Kalgan, and I was worried about our caravan. When we arrived at the rendezvous in the desert, the camels were not there. Neither were there any reports of them from Mongols who had traveled the trail which they should have followed. But after a week, Merin, the leader, rode into camp on his big white camel. The caravan was close behind. The Mongols arrived, gleeful as children to be safe with us. Hearing that there was a band of five hundred brigands ahead of him, Merin had slipped off into the desert. He had traveled only at night, from well to well, and camped during the day in sheltered hollows where he could not easily be seen. His weather-tanned face simply beamed as he told how he had played hide-and-seek with the bandits and yet filled the stomachs of his camels with some of the best grazing they had had all winter.

Bandits on the Road

A short time later, on the way back to Kalgan for some extra supplies, I had an amusing experience with brigands. We had two cars. I drove one and MacKenzie Young the other. Mine was a couple of miles in advance when I came to a deep valley where two Russian cars had been robbed only a week earlier. The bandits had taken twenty thousand dollars' worth of sable skins and killed one man. The other had been stripped naked and left to find his way to Kalgan in his birthday suit.

Just before reaching the spot, I thought: "I wonder if there is any chance of my being held up. Lightning doesn't strike twice in the same place, but brigands might." A moment later I saw the head and shoulders of a man on horseback just showing over the summit of a hill. The sun glinted on a rifle barrel. There were only two kinds of men who carried rifles in China — bandits and soldiers — and, at that time, the two were synonymous. Anyway, I had no mind to have him there, whoever he was. I dropped a bullet from my .38 revolver too close for comfort, but didn't try to hit him. He disappeared abruptly. Just then my car swept over the rim of the basin and started down the steep slope. In the bottom, two hundred yards away, were four horsemen, rifles on their backs. They were bandits and I was in for it.

The trail was narrow and rocky and I couldn't turn; but I knew that a Mongol pony never would stand against the charge of a motor. Opening the cutout, I stepped on the accelerator and the car rushed down the hill roaring like an airplane. The ponies went mad with fright. At first the bandits tried to get the rifles off their backs, but in a moment their chief concern was to stay in their saddles. Three of the ponies rushed across the valley, rearing and plunging madly. The fourth seemed too frightened to run. I slowed up beside him, and will never forget the look of abject terror on the face of that Chinese brigand. It would have been easy to kill him, but there was no sense in doing that. He wore a peaked Mongol hat, and I fired at it four or five times, trying to knock it off his head. Finally his pony started after the others, with me right behind yelling and shooting. It was a regular Wild West Show. When we reached the rim of the valley, I let him go. All four of them got the fright of their lives and I had a lot of fun. When I reported the incident to the commander of a detachment of Chinese soldiers fifty miles farther on, he was furious because I hadn't killed at least one of the bandits. I told him, however, that I was a peaceable explorer. It was his business to kill brigands and not mine.

The second expedition was as successful as the first had been. I have already related how we traveled across the desert to the Flaming Cliffs and found the first dinosaur eggs. Then we pushed westward into new country, mapping a large blank area and making important discoveries in every branch of science. At the end of the season, as we were on our way home, Professor Osborn joined the expedition just north of Kalgan. The last night, our camp was in an amphitheater surrounded by grassy hills. After dinner, the professor and I sat for an hour in front of my tent discussing the future of the expedition. It was obvious that our job could not be completed in the five years originally planned. Ten years was necessary. That meant I must return to America to raise another quarter of a million dollars. Moreover, it was highly desirable that some of our staff go back to study and evaluate the work already done. We determined, therefore, to declare a recess in the field operations for a year, and start anew in 1925.

Just as we were going to bed, a dramatic incident happened that gave the professor a great thrill. Because our camp was in the bandit-infested grasslands of Inner Mongolia, I posted a sentry who was to be relieved every two hours. The candles were hardly out when the man ran in to tell me that he heard horses. I passed the word. When four Chinese rode up, armed with rifles, they were quietly surrounded by all the men of the expedition. I ordered the visitors off their horses. Of course, they professed to be soldiers watching the frontier, but obviously they were bandits expecting easy pickings from a defenseless caravan. We collected their rifles and put them under guard. In the morning we released them, but kept their guns.

"These," I said, "you can get by going to the military post at Chang Peh-hsien. We will leave them with the commander of the garrison." When we reached there, the colonel told me the four men were well-known bandits. He was very unhappy that we had not brought them in along with their rifles. A dozen soldiers, mounted on fast ponies, set out immediately, caught the men, and shot them before the week ended. Within a month after returning to Peking, I sailed for Seattle.

The Great Dinosaur Egg Auction

Dinosaur eggs! Dinosaur eggs! That was all I heard during eight months in America. There was no getting away from the phrase. Vainly did I try to tell of the other, vastly more important, discoveries of the expedition. No one was interested. No one even listened. Eventually, I became philosophical, as Stefanssen did about his blond Eskimos. After all, the situation had its bright side. I had returned to raise a quarter of a million dollars and the publicity was of great assistance. I might as well take advantage of it. How to do it? The people who had given the first two hundred fifty thousand were pleased. Some of them, like Mr. Morgan, Mr. Baker, Mr. Rockefeller and half a dozen others, continued their original subscriptions. That helped, but it was far from enough. The money was coming in too slowly for my peace of mind.

I was living with Professor Osborn at the time, and one morning said to him at breakfast:

"I'm convinced the general public would help finance the expedition, but they think small contributions aren't wanted. They believe this is only a rich man's show. If we could auction off one dinosaur egg, as a contribution to the expedition's funds, it would give grand publicity. Every news story could explain that small contributions are more than welcome."

The professor was just drinking a cup of coffee. He set it down suddenly. "Roy, it's a great idea. A ten-strike. Let's do it."

Thus started the "Great Dinosaur Egg Auction." A call went to the reporters to meet at four o'clock in my office. Forty or more came. I told them frankly just why we were doing it and asked for help.

"We'll sell the egg to the highest bidder. The proceeds will go to the finances of the expedition. Please stress in all your stories that it's up to the public if we are to be able to continue our explorations. Any contributions are welcome. I'll give you a report each day about what bids are received. They ought to make good stories." The newsmen figuratively licked their chops. They knew a lot of good copy would result.

The day after the announcement, the *Illustrated London News* cabled an offer of two thousand dollars for the egg. The National Geographic Society upped it to three thousand. A museum in Australia bid thirty-five hundred. Yale University offered four thousand. The publicity was enormous, and, true to their promise, the newspapermen tacked a plea for money to all the stories. Checks began to come in by every mail. Ten, twenty-five, fifty, a hundred dollars. Many were for only a dollar; one was for ten thousand! By the time the auction ended, and Mr. Austin Colgate had purchased the egg for five thousand dollars as a gift to Colgate University, we had garnered fifty thousand dollars in public contributions.

I was very pleased, but it proved to be a boomerang. Nothing else so disastrous ever happened to the expedition. Up to this time, the Chinese and Mongols had taken us at face value. Now they thought we were making money out of our explorations. We had found about thirty eggs. If one was sold for five thousand dollars, the whole lot must be valued at one hundred fifty thousand. They read about the other fossils — dinosaurs, titanotheres, *Baluchitherium!* Probably, these, too, were worth their weight in gold. Why should the Mongols and the Chinese let us have such priceless treasures for nothing? I had to combat this idea throughout all the remaining years of the expedition.

The assumption was natural, I suppose. They couldn't understand that the five thousand dollars was a fictitious value, engendered by publicity. Moreover, that any purely scientific or art object has a market value of only what it can be sold for to someone who has a special reason for possessing it. As an example, when it came to insuring the eggs on the trip across the Pacific, the only money value we could decide upon was what the expedition of that year had cost to get them. Of course, the eggs were studied immediately and the results published. Dr. Victor van Strallen, in Brussels, the greatest world authority on fossil eggs, did a very thorough job. At once their value dropped somewhat, for the scientific cream had been skimmed. As a matter of fact, a year later I asked the director of the British Museum in London what he would pay for one.

"Well," he said, "I should hesitate to offer more than a hundred pounds. They have been studied. Now their chief value lies in exhibition. You have been kind enough to give us a cast which no one could tell from the original without close examination. No, I don't think I'd give more than a hundred pounds."

It wasn't quite as simple as that, but still there were elements of truth in what he said. By the same token, one might argue that a copy of a letter written by Shakespeare was as good as the original. But perhaps the director thought I needed the money and was hoping he might get a bargain! I forgot to say that we had distributed casts of the eggs to most of the large museums of the world as a gift from the expedition.

Shortly after returning to New York, the Lord tempted

me apropos of eggs. One of the biggest novelty manufacturers in the world came to my office with a letter of introduction from a prominent New York banker.

"I," said he, "have a great plan. It will mean a lot of money for both of us. We'll make casts of the dinosaur egg; use them as paperweights, desk sets, etc., with your signature on the bottom. The original Easter egg! That's the idea. The first edition will be a million copies. I'll flood the world through my distributing agents. You can have a royalty. Most of them will sell cheap. Sell for seventy-five cents. They'll go like hot cakes. I'm not guessing. I know. It's my business to know what'll sell. You'll make a quarter of a million dollars or I'm a Chinaman. Here's a contract. You have your lawyer look it over, and I'll give you twenty thousand dollars advance royalty the day it's signed. Must get at it immediately. We ought to start production in two weeks."

It was a bit breath-taking. Attractive, perhaps, but even at first thought I didn't like it. Of course, the money would be used to continue our explorations, but everyone would think it went into my pocket. Moreover, the expedition would be stamped as a commercial venture in the eyes of the world. Science camouflaging business! Professor Osborn agreed with me. I've always been glad the offer was refused.

That winter I did eighty-one lectures in eighty days in almost every state of the Union. At the end of it I felt, and looked, like a sucked orange. But there was something more than three hundred thousand dollars in the expedition "kitty" when I went off to China.

In the Gobi Again

The 1925 expedition was the largest, and most ambitious, of the series. In fact, it was too large, I discovered, for completely effective work. Fifty men all told; eight motors, and one hundred fifty camels. It took so much food, so much gear, and so many cars to handle the big party that our mobility was somewhat reduced. Nevertheless, it proved to be the most successful season.

In general it was similar to the first two. New country explored, new areas mapped, new fossil deposits opened. Greater difficulties from the changed political conditions required tact and force at times. Bandits were a nuisance, but in two or three very lively "incidents" we lost no men. The number of sciences represented had been increased to seven. We had become greatly interested in the climate of Mongolia during successive geological periods, and wished to check our deductions with the study of fossil plants and insects as well as from geology and paleontology. Osborn's original thesis that Central Asia was a great center of origin and distribution of northern animal life had been demonstrated pretty clearly. But other important facts emerged. The Central Asia plateau was the oldest continuously dry land in the world. For a hundred and fifty million years it had been rising, while Europe and America in part had successively risen and sunk below the sea. Thus Central Asia gave an unbroken record of animal life such as existed nowhere else in the world. Mongolia never had experienced an invasion of ice, as did Europe and America. There were climatic cycles, wet and dry, wet and dry; also cycles within cycles. These fascinating problems made the year's work important far beyond the limits of pure paleontology. The accuracy of our maps, too, never had been approached in former explorations.

At the Flaming Cliffs we found more dinosaur eggs — bigger and better eggs! Also there came a fortnight of intense excitement when a new human culture was discovered in the basin less than half a mile from camp. It was an area of shifting sand blown into dunes against the stems of twisted tamarisk trees. Sculptured red bluffs marked the entrance to shallow valleys floored with sandstone, where the wind had swept the loose sediment away.

On the clean hard surface of the rock, pointed cores, tiny rounded scrapers, delicately worked drills, and arrowheads of red jasper, slate, chalcedony and churt were scattered like newly fallen snow. Among them were bits of dinosaur eggshell drilled with neat round holes — evidently used as a necklace by some primitive debutante. Also pieces of crude pottery. It was a strange jumble of conflicting specimens, some indicating an Old Stone Age culture, others dating it much later. For two weeks all the scientists of the expedition concentrated on the problem. Night after night, sitting around the campfire of tamarisk branches, we discussed every detail and every theory pro and con. Eventually the solution emerged clearly, but the archaeologist alone would have been hopelessly stymied. It was a wonderful example of the value of correlated work on the spot. The solution was this. The site had been used continuously by human beings for many thousands of years. The oldest culture was late Paleolithic, or Old Stone Age; then came a transition stage, Mesolithic, which gradually developed into the Neolithic, or New Stone Age.

[233   ]

A problem was to determine where our people fitted into the mosaic of primitive European humans, if they did. As a matter of fact, their relationship was only relative, for they represented an entirely new race with a culture distinctly their own, most closely allied to the Azilians of France and Spain. We named them the "Dune Dwellers." They roamed over all Mongolia ten to twenty thousand years ago. Dressed in skins, probably living under rude shelters of hides or bushes, they hunted, fought, and loved much as do the primitive savages of Australia and Tasmania today. Later, Dune Dweller implements were found in Alaska. One site is on the campus of the University of Alaska. These people must have migrated to America by way of the Bering Strait and may be among the oldest inhabitants of this country.

There was another great discovery at the Flaming Cliffs during that summer of 1925. In our first year's collection, Granger had labeled a tiny skull "unidentified reptile," for the deposit was the Cretaceous at the end of the Age of Reptiles. Eventually, the skull was freed from rock and proved to be one of the earliest-known *mammals*. In more than a hundred years of paleontology, only a single fragmentary skull of a mammal from the Age of Reptiles ever had been discovered. That was *Tritylodon* of South Africa. The British Museum considered it to be the world's greatest paleontological treasure. At the Flaming Cliffs we found *seven skulls and parts of skeletons* of these Mesozoic mammals. They were tiny creatures, not larger than a rat, that crawled about under the feet of dinosaurs at the close of the Age of Reptiles, seventy or more million years ago. After the dinosaur eggs have been forgotten, these little skulls will be remembered by scientists as the *crowning single discovery of our paleontological research in Asia.*

We left the Flaming Cliffs with regret. They had given us more than we dared to hope for from the entire Gobi: dinosaur eggs, a hundred skulls and skeletons of unknown dinosaurs, seven Mesozoic mammals and the new Dune Dweller human culture, to say nothing of lesser discoveries. As my car climbed the steep slope to the eastern rim, I stopped for a last look into the vast red basin. I would never see it again. "Never" is a long word, but I knew that for the last time my caravan had fought its way across the desolate reaches of the Gobi to this treasure vault of world history.

A Plague of Snakes

We were driven out of our final camp of the season by a plague of snakes. A pit viper is the only poisonous snake in the desert. Our tents were pitched on a promontory with steep rocky sides. During the night, the temperature dropped to freezing and the vipers came up to get warm. Norman Lovell was lying in bed when he saw a wriggling form cross the triangular patch of moonlight in his tent door. He was about to get up and kill the snake, when he decided to have a look before putting his bare feet on the ground. About each of the legs of his camp cot a viper was coiled. Reaching for a collector's pickax, he disposed of the two snakes which had hoped to share his bed. Then began a still hunt for the first arrival. He was hardly out of his sleeping bag, when the grandfather of all vipers crawled from under a gasoline box near the head of his cot.

[235]

Lovell was having rather a lively evening of it, but he was not alone. Morris killed five vipers in his tent and Wang found a snake coiled in his shoe. Then he picked up his soft cap from the ground and a viper fell out of that. Dr. Loucks actually put his hand on one under a pile of shotgun cases. Forty-seven snakes were killed that night. Fortunately, the cold made them sluggish, and they were slow to strike. But it got on our nerves and everyone became decidedly jumpy. The Chinese and Mongols deserted their tents, sleeping in the cars and on camel boxes. The rest of us never moved after dark without a flashlight and pickax. When I walked out of the tent one evening, I stepped on something soft and round. My yell brought out the whole camp, but it was only a coil of rope. A few moments later Walter Granger made a vicious lunge with his pick, shouting:

"I got you that time!" But Walter had merely sliced a pipe cleaner!

The new camp proved to be as rich in fossils as in reptiles, but at last the snakes won. Moreover, flurries of snow warned us to be on our way southward. On September 12th, the cars roared down the slope to the basin floor, leaving Viper Camp to the snakes and vultures. The 1925 expedition was ended.

Panic in Peking

The years 1926–1927 marked a turning point in the history of modern China. It was important, too, in the fortunes of the Central Asiatic Expedition. Antiforeignism burst into flame out of the still-smoldering fires of the Boxer Rebellion of 1900. Chiang Kai-shek, in command of his Yangtze Valley army, was energetically making plans to attack Chang Tso-lin, dictator of the North, with the object of bringing the entire country under the control of his party. He was ably assisted by the Communist Borodin, and Russian generals directed his army. It had remarkable success and eventually moved on Shanghai with the avowed intention of taking that city, ousting the foreigners, and claiming the port for the Chinese.

At Shanghai, barbed-wire entanglements were erected and the International Settlement put under martial law. One or two clashes took place, with considerable loss to the Chinese, but no determined attack was launched against the concessions. All foreign legations ordered their nationals from the interior of China. Reports were continually arriving of murder and outrages committed on foreigners in various parts of the country. It was a repetition of events leading up to the Boxer Rebellion of 1900, only on a larger scale.

For the first time, I saw something like a panic in Peking. The Southerners were pushing slowly northward, and all legations advised their nationals to leave Peking. Most of the women and children went to Darien or Manila. As for the expedition, we had a carefully thought-out plan for the protection of the headquarters. With machine guns posted on the roofs, we would be able to present a pretty strong defense against looters, or even well-armed soldiery. All the staff offered to remain with me. I told the American Minister that we were not going to leave our house and valuable equipment; that was flat. I would absolve the legation from responsibility for our safety.

Suddenly the situation was completely changed. Marshal Chang Tso-lin made a dramatic raid on the Dal Bank and the Russian military attaché's office next to the Soviet Embassy in the walled Legation Quarter. The raid took place at eleven o'clock in the morning, with the unofficial permission of the Diplomatic Body. I happened to be at the National City Bank on the opposite side of the street, and witnessed the entire proceeding. It was most spectacular and totally unexpected. Even in his wildest dreams Chang Tso-lin could not have believed that the results would be so important. The Bolsheviks had depended upon the diplomatic immunity of the Embassy, and used it as a central clearing house from which operations were conducted all over the world. Raids that subsequently took place in London, Paris, and the Argentine were made upon information obtained at the Soviet Embassy in Peking. Chang Tso-lin then set to work systematically to rid North China of Communists. Those Chinese who were caught in the Russian Embassy raid were slowly and scientifically strangled in front of the Old Marshal himself. Each one took twenty minutes to die. Hardly a day passed that one or more persons were not executed at the public ground opposite the Temple of Heaven. Most had their heads chopped off. A few privileged ones were shot.

I had gone to Shanghai after the raid, but had an urgent message from the American Minister to return to Peking. Marshal Chang Tso-lin asked me as a neutral — and one who knew how to do a book — to select and edit the captured documents for world distribution, a sort of "White Book." I declined with regret. It would have been intensely interesting, but I was an explorer, not a politician.

Antiforeignism Interrupts Our Work

The prospect of continuing our explorations in Mongolia in 1926 – 1927 could not have been blacker. We proceeded to liquidate certain effects of the expedition, put others in a place of safety, and reduce current expenses to the minimum. All the staff, except MacKenzie Young, I sent back to America. He remained with me to watch events and prepare for an expedition in 1928, if it were possible. In Peking conditions settled down to normal with amazing rapidity after the Soviet Embassy raid. War, of course, was still going on in Central China — but then, there was always war! So long as it didn't come knocking at our front door, it was only of academic interest.

What with polo, social events, and a good deal of magazine writing, the summer and autumn of 1927 passed quickly for Mac Young and me. We purchased a new caravan of camels, got food and equipment packed, and cabled for the staff to come. The expedition of 1928 was successful in a new part of Inner Mongolia, but antiforeignism made it difficult on our return.

We were able to do another expedition in 1930, but then the political situation became impossible, and I decided to end the work, even though we had only scratched the surface of the Gobi.

This unfortunate antiforeignism in China stopped short a dream which had begun to develop in my mind much as did the Central Asiatic expeditions. It would have been something bigger and vastly more important than anything we had done in our restricted explorations. My dream was to establish an "International Institute for Asiatic Research."

I discussed the plan with scientific societies in England, France, Sweden, Denmark, and Germany. Everyone was enthusiastic. I already had the pledge of a million dollars as an initial endowment, but China's antiforeignism made it impossible. The plan calls for a Utopian state of international cooperation, to be sure, but I do not think this is too much to hope for in the future. It would be a "United Nations of Science."

The job ahead of me in the summers of 1931 and 1932 was to write the narrative volume of the Central Asiatic Expedition's final reports. Even though our work in the Gobi was prematurely ended, the book could best be done in China away from the turmoil of New York. Out of the funds available for each year's exploration, I had set aside a part for publication. No other big expedition had ever done that. Usually, at the end of their explorations, they have to shop around to get money for publication, and it is exceedingly difficult. Fieldwork is soon forgotten. Only the publications remain as a permanent record of achievement. At the end of our first expedition the results began to appear in short papers. New species were described; new facts put on record. A hundred and forty-five papers have been published. A series of quarto final volumes was projected under the general title *The Natural History of Central Asia*. Seven are completed, and I look at them with pride. As long as science exists they will stand as the *Systema Natura* of Mongolia.

Moreover, our general map of Mongolia was completed and printed by the United States War Department for its own use during World War II. It is the only accurate map of that country.

Writing the narrative volume became the real point of my life. Social activities for me were out. No luncheons, dinners, or cocktail parties. Peking knew me no more as a host. I was a night worker and enjoyed it. By the end of the summer of 1932 the book was finished. It runs to six hundred and seventy-eight pages and is about the size of Webster's Unabridged Dictionary. Title: *New Conquest of Central Asia.*

Good-by to China

One day in October I wrote "The End" on the manuscript. No longer was there reason to maintain a home in China. For twelve years I had lived in the great house at No. 2 Kung-hsien Hutung. It had become something personal to me, a part of my very self. When, for the last time, I walked through the big red gates, tears were in my eyes and I was unashamed.

My wife and I had parted company in Paris in 1930. So I made a new home for myself in New York in a lovely little penthouse atop the roof of the Hotel des Artistes. The trustees made me vice director of the American Museum, in charge of exploration. I also became president of the Explorers Club of New York, of which I had been a member since 1908. They gave me the Explorers Medal. Since it was awarded by my own colleagues I value it highly. I should have been happy, but I wasn't. I longed to get back to the desert. So in 1933 I went to Europe and planned a long expedition to Chinese and Russian Turkestan, to go in from India.

Professor Osborn had retired after twenty-five years as president of the museum, and F. Trubee Davison had taken his place. We were old friends, and I knew I would have his full cooperation in the new explorations.

Then a turn of fate changed my whole life. I was sitting in my office when a secretary rushed in to say that the director, Dr. George Sherwood, was very ill. It was a heart attack and the doctors said he must have six months complete rest. The trustees asked me to become acting director until he recovered. It was something interesting and constructive. All my restlessness vanished.

Fate was very busy in my behalf at that time. I met a girl — Wilhelmina Christmas — "Billie" everyone called her. I had built up a philosophy of life in which marriage never again would figure. It was all very clear and logical until I met Billie. Then the theory collapsed of its own weight. We were married three months later.

It became evident that Dr. Sherwood could not resume his duties as director of the museum, and the trustees asked me to take the post. I was not keen to accept, for I knew it would mean giving up exploration. Still, that I should become director of the institution with which I had been connected ever since graduating from college was a logical conclusion. Moreover, things of consuming interest was happening in the museum. African Hall, the dream of my old friend Carl Akeley was nearing completion. October, 1935, saw the opening of the Hayden Planetarium, and plans were under way for a Hall of North American Mammals. Life was not monotonous. Every prominent visitor to the city was brought to the American Museum, as the greatest institution of its kind in the world. Al Smith got them first at the Empire State Building; then they came to us. We had the Great and the Near Great, Royalty and semi-Royalty, and the ordinary public, who were more interesting but didn't make the headlines. Nearly two million people passed through the museum doors every year. It was an inspiring job.

But I did not react well to the confinement in an office and the carbon monoxide of a city. For twenty-eight years

I had lived in the field, and I was like a wild animal that had been trapped late in life and put in a comfortable cage. Physiologically and psychologically I couldn't adjust myself to the change.

In 1937, Billie and I bought Pondwood Farm, in Connecticut, as a week-end place, and had a thrilling time cutting it out of the wilderness. Billie, who is much wiser than I, saw the handwriting on the wall, and two years later we rebuilt the house as a permanent home. In 1941, Trubee Davison was given a leave of absence and went to Washington as aide to General Emmons in the Air Corps. That was a sad blow to me, personally. My job in the museum had become almost entirely financial — raising money to meet an ever-increasing deficit in the yearly budget. I wasn't happy. I felt it was not fair either to the museum or myself to continue as director. So I offered my resignation to the board of trustees, to take effect January 1, 1942, and was appointed honorary director.

I may be pardoned for quoting an editorial in the *New York Times* published on November 12, 1941, when my resignation was announced:

DR. ANDREWS RESIGNS

It is seldom that a man leaves his work because he is in love with it. Yet this is the reason for the resignation of Roy Chapman Andrews as director of the Museum of Natural History. World chaos has narrowed the field of exploration in which he served the Museum for so many years and at the same time forced the institution to deal with new financial problems for the solution of which Dr. Andrews says he is not particularly fitted "either by inclination, temperament or training." So he steps aside to let someone else conserve the results of the period of expansion in which he was the prime mover.

For that period he was the ideal man. In the Asiatic desert, on the ice ridges of the Arctic or along the ocean wastes he developed an unfailing gift for dramatizing his scientific adventures. It was he who brought back the fossil dinosaur eggs, pursued the elusive Dawn Man and tracked down the *Baluchitherium*, that giant among all prehistoric mammals. He not only made the Museum a vital force in scientific education but brought the public flocking to it, because people found its colorful halls one of the most fascinating vistas in the city scene. For thirty-five years, more than half his life, Dr. Andrews has lived with and for the Museum. It should reassure his successor to know from his letter to the trustees that his talent and enthusiasm will be given freely for the remainder of his life.

Billie and I went to live at Pondwood Farm. It lies in the foothills of the Berkshires, in the northwest corner of Connecticut. The picture window in our living room looks out upon a six-acre pond; there is a trout stream at the bottom of our hill; two bass lakes of the Doolittle Club almost adjoin our property; woodcock and grouse covers are at the front door. I have a balanced program of work and play. Write in the morning; fish or shoot in the afternoon! Summers at Pondwood; winters in Tucson, Arizona. My friends say I am lucky. I know damned well I am!

Such is a kaleidoscopic picture of my life up to the Year of Our Lord 1954. I loved living it, and it is fun writing about it. Always there has been an adventure just around the corner — and the world is still full of corners!